RETIREMENT PLANNING MADE EASY

A simple yet powerful step-by-step
approach to a safer, more secure
retirement income

DIANE MARRA, RFC

Legal Disclaimer

The Publisher and the Author make no representations or warranties with respect to the accuracy or completeness of the contents of this work, and specifically disclaim all warranties, including without limitation warranties for a particular purpose. No warranty may be created or extended by sales or promotional materials. The advice and strategies contained herein may not be suitable for every situation.

Neither the publisher nor the author shall be liable for damages arising herefrom. The fact that an organization or website is referred to in this work as a citation and/or a potential source of further information does not mean that the author or the publisher endorses the information the organization or website it may provide or recommendations it may make.

Further, readers should be aware that Internet websites listed in this work may have changed or disappeared between when this work was written and when it is read.

Investment advisory services offered through Horter Investment Management, LLC, a SEC-Registered Investment Adviser. Horter Investment Management does not provide legal or tax advice. Investment Adviser Representatives of Horter Investment Management may only conduct business with residents of the states and jurisdictions in which they are properly registered. Insurance and annuity products are sold separately through Diane Marra. Securities transactions for Horter Investment Management clients are placed through Trust Company of America, TD Ameritrade, Pershing Advisor Solutions, Jefferson National Life Insurance Company, Security Benefit Life Insurance Company and ED&F Man Capital Markets.

ISBN: 978-0-9972217-0-1

Dedicated to:

My husband, Paul,
and my children,
Ashley, Tyler and Jaclyn

&

My parents, George and Audrey Johnson,
who encouraged me to take up a career
in the financial industry

Contents

Introduction:
Planning For Retirement Income Stability

Retirement has, in some ways, become an unfriendly word. With so many changing elements, it can be hard to know if you have done enough for a comfortable retirement. With the government introducing changes such as the Affordable Care Act and ever-changing tax provisions, the financial landscape can be difficult to keep up with. It's safe to say that even those who were once firmly grounded in financial education are often struggling through a quagmire of hidden laws, minor details, and potentially damaging clauses.

More than ever it has become essential for people planning their retirement, and those already greeting their retirement days, to have reliable financial advice to guide them through the maze of detailed planning that will be necessary to achieve a comfortable degree of success. Thinking that your retirement income is enough, and *strategically planning* for it to be enough, are two very different things!

It's a sad reality that many baby boomers who are now reaching their retirement years will not have enough to fall back on. According to the Employee Benefit Research Institute, some 46% of American workers have less than $10,000 saved up for retirement. Even worse, 29% of the workforce has less than $1000 saved.

With savings at an all-time low, and the demand for financial literacy so high, it's easy to see how important retirement planning has really become for the average person. Many people are unaware of the changes that should be made when moving from an accumulation phase to a distribution phase. The focus should be on constructing a low-risk, low-volatility retirement income plan that will help provide them with the stable income they need for the rest of their lives.

Doing this safely and without subjecting your life savings to undue risk can be an impossibility without good and accurate information. When the financial field is so littered with bad practices and unaccountable brokers, how do you—the authentically motivated consumer—ensure that your retirement will be safe, secure and sustainable for the long haul?

Once retirement is on the horizon, many of the rules that you've followed while accumulating your pot of gold will need to be suspended. If you take the time to educate yourself even a little bit, your efforts will likely be greatly rewarded, generating lasting results. This education can (and often does) make the difference between success and failure.

The risks in retirement are real, and they can be devastating. Imagine yourself running out of money some years into your retirement. Imagine suddenly being stripped of the income that you believed was secure, simply because of an overlooked technicality. It can and does happen to people every day. If you discount the value of adequate retirement planning, somewhere down the road, you, as well as your family, may be paying the piper.

This book will walk you through procedures and ideas for preparing and setting up a plan, help you protect yourself from devastating pitfalls, and will offer strategies for safely managing your retirement income.

Chapter 1:
The Keys to a Successful Retirement Income Strategy

"Preparation for old age should begin no later than one's teens. A life which is empty of purpose until 65 will not suddenly become filled on retirement."
—DWIGHT L. MOODY

The New Retirement Landscape

The "boom" in baby boomer retirement is on the rise. This mass stampede towards retirement runs alongside a notoriously unstable time in America.

The world we live in has become complicated and challenging to navigate. The retirement environment today includes low interest rates, volatile stock markets around the world, unprecedented longevity, increasing budget deficits and financial ambiguity. These unfortunate realities are creating unnecessary stress and anxiety in many lives.

Planning for retirement is not going to be as easy as it was for your parents. I'm not sure if companies give out gold watches anymore. I do know that guaranteed pensions are far and few between. Today, much more preparation will be necessary for a successful outcome.

On a personal note, I have heard some deeply troubling stories about retirement plans gone wrong, as I'm sure you have. None of us want to end up being a financial burden on our families during our retirement years. Running out of money is a very real possibility for those who don't take the time to prepare for retirement.

Personal Responsibility and Your Retirement Portfolio

Personal Responsibility Defined: The willingness to accept the importance of societal standards for individual behavior, and to make strenuous personal efforts to live by those standards. No one but you is to blame for your retirement planning, or lack thereof, so make it count!

Baby boomers are facing a crisis—the first generation to ever live through times like these. Whereas once you could trust Social Security and your company retirement plan to secure a long and happy retirement, this is no longer the case. We have entered into an era of personal responsibility.

Employer retirement benefits have become much less significant over the past few decades. Only 20% of workers from the private sector will have access to a pension that pays out for life. When 401Ks came on scene, they were was supposed to *supplement* the company pension. Now, for many, the 401K *is* the pension plan and *you* are responsible for funding it, choosing the best investments, and making sure that the money lasts appropriately. As a result, many boomers are realizing that they are not prepared.

It's also been said that the Social Security system is fundamentally flawed. In fact, the Social Security (OASDI) Trustees Report states that "significant uncertainty" surrounds the "best estimates" of future circumstances. It's up to you to make your economic security in retirement a personal mission.

We have an industry bursting with "rock-star" financial brokers who place the financial futures of their clients in a "one size fits all" strategy. Maybe they lack competence or understanding, but this doesn't work.

When the stock market has a drawdown of 50% and half your portfolio has evaporated, the answer I most often hear my clients getting from their brokers is "don't worry, it will come back, everyone lost money."

That just isn't true. "Everyone" doesn't lose money. For me, that's an unacceptable answer. It's a put-off and in my opinion it's callous. With knowledge and genuine concern, portfolios most certainly can be protected from large downside risk.

People quite often have no idea how or why their current portfolio was constructed and invested the way it is. I find that many have no real interest in investing their life savings in a highly volatile stock market, but on the advice of "reliable" brokers, a large portion of their savings is subjected to very high risk. Ask anyone who was invested in the stock market as recently as 2008 how that feels.

As you enter retirement, you should understand that ultimately you have to assume ownership of your retirement portfolio, investments, and the income streams you hope to achieve. You'll need a sustainable plan that has the potential to generate reliable income for the rest of your life. That's the best way to ensure your success.

That's not to say that you have to get an entire education in Financial and Retirement Income Planning. Of course not! It took me many years to gain this kind of financial and retirement knowledge.

What it does mean is that you should take some time to educate yourself enough so that you can understand the procedures involved in sustainable retirement income planning. Reading this book is one step. You may want to enlist the help of a qualified financial advisor who specializes in retirement distribution planning.

A significant aspect of a planner's experience lies in the asset accumulation phase. Accumulating money while you're working, and building a plan of distribution in retirement, are two very different disciplines. I'll get into that in greater detail later on.

The right person will help you gain a basic knowledge of the process, and help you design a plan that can generate reliable income that you can presumably count on for the rest of your life.

The last thing you want to do is decide that you don't know enough, stick your head in the sand, and hand the whole process off to someone else, with no understanding of how and why your portfolio is designed the way it is. Be proactive about the hows and the whys of your portfolio design. Ask questions.

You may have been working with someone for a number of years, and feel that you know them quite well. You may be comfortable, and it's easier than starting a new relationship. I understand that, but be sure that you understand that planner's knowledge base regarding distribution planning before you head off to the golf course. Otherwise, you risk being extremely disappointed when it's too late to do anything about it.

Moving From Accumulation to Distribution

One of the most important things that you have on your side when you begin saving money for retirement is *time*. When you are 30, 40, even 50 years away from retirement, you can afford to take more risk with the way you invest your money. You want to accumulate as much as you can so that you will be able to generate a paycheck when you're no longer employed.

When you're working and putting money aside on a consistent basis, you're performing a strategy called "Dollar Cost Averaging." Dollar cost averaging actually works quite well while you are in the accumulation phase. Because you're adding money on a weekly or monthly basis, sometimes you're buying high and sometimes you're buying low (assuming you are invested in the stock market or some instrument related to it).

This averages things out for you and to some extent reduces your overall risk. It does not, of course, *eliminate* risk. There are many fine and knowledgeable brokers that can help you with this area. However, you will want to find someone who has your best interests at heart.

Hopefully, as you make your way closer to your retirement date, you've moved your portfolio toward less risk. You've spent the last 40 or even 50 years in the workforce. Maybe you've raised a family, owned a few houses, taken some great vacations, and along the way have managed to set aside a few dollars. Maybe you're lucky enough to have a company pension that you'll be able to count on, maybe not. And for now, lucky for us, Social Security is still here.

Or perhaps you're already staring down at the "Golden Years." It came so fast that you've barely even had time to consider how to go about planning it out.

Retirement Income Planning (the orderly and strategically timed distribution of assets in retirement) begins where the accumulation of assets ends. There are many moving parts to designing your plan, and none should be taken lightly or left to chance.

One of the most difficult things for people to change, when they start thinking about retiring, is their mindset when moving from an accumulation phase to a distribution phase.

Many people continue to hold onto the idea that "how much they earn on their money" is most important—and it is, if you're 35 and working and still accumulating assets for retirement.

However, what you *earn on your money* is secondary and much less important once you enter retirement. What is it secondary *to*, you may ask? The safety, security and preservation of the very assets that will generate your income streams for hopefully 25, 30 or 40 years of retirement! If you lose what you have, it cannot generate an income check for you every month and you may find yourself looking for a J.O.B.

This is not to say that you can't do well in retirement. You can, and you can do it with minimal risk! But the distribution of assets over many years, making sure that it doesn't run out before you do, is no easy task.

The very first thing you must come to terms with is that you are no longer in a position of accumulating money, so your philosophy has to change. You cannot leave your money in harm's way, taking risk that simply isn't necessary. Time will be against you at that point. You won't have the time, once you are near or in retirement, to make up a 30% or 40% loss.

When you transition into retirement your risk in many ways sky-rockets. You are no longer working, and the weekly paycheck stops. All of the money that you have saved in your life is now finite. The decisions that you make will impact your quality of life, as well as your family's.

There is an essential shift that should take place with regard to how you handle your assets when you transition into retirement. As you now know, the accumulation phase is concerned with building your retirement nest egg. The ultimate goal is to maximize your investment and savings returns over time. Then, when you reach your chosen retirement age, strategies must change.

As you move into the distribution phase, things get more complicated. You will need to monitor your withdrawal rate. This is extremely important. As an example, if you haven't moved to a safer haven and you are withdrawing 5% or $25,000 per year from a $500,000 portfolio, and that portfolio losses 30%, its value is now $350,000. If you make no adjustments to your withdrawal, that same $25,000 now represents 7.14% of your portfolio. That's a very big difference.

You'll want to take a closer look at taxes and strategies available to reduce them on an ongoing basis. Let's not forget about medical costs, inflation and large ticket items to name a few.

You'll want to consider balancing your investments for a safer, more reliable portfolio. The ultimate goal of a sound retirement plan is to keep your nest egg intact, with enough money to cover seen and unforeseen events for the rest of your days while still maintaining the lifestyle you desire.

Major Risks to Retirement Income

There are six clear risks that are associated with your retirement income. If you are going to correctly and adequately plan your retirement, then you need to take these risk factors into account as early as possible. These are the risks that can lead to the erosion of your retirement capital, which in turn will impact the amount you live on each month.

- *The first risk is related to longevity.* We are living in a time of advanced medicine. I'm sure you've heard it said: "70 is the new 50." Retirement can stretch upwards of 30 years. That's a lot of years to plan for.

- *The second risk is inflation.* It's a fact of life and one financial element that most retirees fear. Inflation can cause your annual income needs to skyrocket, and can devastate your retirement over time. This is something that you must plan for, or you will be subject to dwindling income amounts as your portfolio does not correctly adjust to inflation.

- *The third risk is the expense of healthcare.* Because you'll be older, you will need to ensure that your medical needs are taken care of. It's one of your largest expenses, and one that you cannot plan enough for. One study from the Employee Benefit Research Institute recommends having $227,000 for medical expenses per couple in retirement. My personal experience with my own clients is that it can be quite a bit higher.

- *The fourth major risk is fluctuations related to your investments.* Assuming that your assets are invested in the stock market or some high-risk variation that is affected by it, poor market performance will negatively impact your portfolio as well as your income. If you haven't taken the time to restructure for less risk, this will hurt. You'll have to wait until things turn around and head back up. It can take years upon years just to get back to even, while you're faced with taking a higher percentage of income from a smaller portfolio.

- *The fifth major risk is related to taxes.* When taxes go up, your income goes down.

- *The sixth major risk is related to public policy and legal changes.* As a kid my siblings and I would play board games such as Monopoly. Everything would be going along just fine until an older sibling came along and joined in. Minutes after the newcomer joined, she would decide she didn't like the rules we were playing by and would change them. We followed along, of course, because we were smaller and younger. Suddenly, instead of owning nine properties (Boardwalk and Park Place included) and a wad of cash, I was broke. No money and all my properties either foreclosed or sold at a deep discount! We had no choice, no control.

Public policy changes, in my opinion, can produce scenarios remarkably similar—but with far more dire consequences than a child's game.

You might design and implement the best retirement plan around the current legal structure. Suddenly, the government decides to change the rules. You will have no choice but to change with it and adapt. We have absolutely no direct control over public policy and legal changes.

Three potential public policy changes you may want to keep a lookout for:

1. Required Minimum Distributions for ROTH IRAs, which currently have no minimum distributions for owners.

2. A cap on wealth inside IRAs.

3. Reduction of Social Security Benefits, increased taxes to fund benefits, another extension of full retirement age, and elimination of certain claiming strategies people use to maximize benefits. You can research this yourself at ssa.gov/budget. These changes will have a huge impact on planning strategies if they come to pass.

All of these risks (and more) need to be accounted for in retirement income planning. They are the main causes for reduction of retirement income buying power. There is nothing we can do to eliminate them, but it's imperative that we plan for them as best we can.

Longevity and health care costs are related risks

Americans are living longer. The need for health care and long-term care, whether in a facility or at home, will continue to increase among retired Americans. The high costs and unpredictability of health care needs make these especially important risk factors to account for.

Health care costs: Health care costs are among the fastest-growing expenses among retirees.

Long-term care needs: An unexpected long-term care event can force an individual to enter retirement early.

A survey of pre-retirees and retirees ages 55-75 found that health care and long-term care expenses together account for 12-15% of retirement expenses, depending on the household income. Today, the average annual cost of a health-care aid who works in your home eight hours per day is slightly more than $60,000 per year.

A 2010 study estimates that health care costs for a retired couple age 65 could amount, on average, to $250,000 over the course of their retirement years. This figure does not include long-term care costs.

Longer life spans also increase the challenge by requiring that your assets last 15, 25, 35 years or longer. Uncertain taxes and inflation can undermine even the most well-thought-out and well-implemented plans.

And 55% of retirees surveyed said they retired earlier than planned. 39% were forced to retire due to health issues or job loss.

The Recap

At the end of every chapter, there will be a helpful recap section like this one, to help you make sense of the information that has been shared with you in the chapter you have just read. Use this section to raise the right questions with your chosen financial provider.

- **The state of retirement income planning is in flux.**

  We live in a volatile, uncertain world. Baby boomers need a consistent income that is safe and secure with reduced risk. But the landscape has changed. Employer retirement plans are a thing of the past and Social Security may be uncertain. More than ever before, retirees are dependent upon their investments to generate retirement income. It's your responsibility to seek out a reliable strategy that will suit your needs. Don't allow your portfolio to retain high-risk investments. Losses can significantly reduce your income and devastate your retirement.

- **"You don't have to see the whole staircase, just take the first step." (Martin Luther King)**

  Take personal responsibility for the outcome of your retirement. Enlist the help of an advisor who specializes in retirement income planning and educate yourself enough to understand and take control of your retirement income, even if you have help.

- **The accumulation phase and the distribution phase of retrement planning are entirely different, require different strtaegies and different mindsets.**

  What you earn on your money (return) is secondary once you enter retirement. The safety, security and preservation of the assets that will generate your income streams for hopefully 30 or 40 years of retirement becomes your priority. You can take less risk and still do very well in retirement.

- **There's no such thing as too much planning.**

  Make sure you plan for the risks that can sneak up and devastate your retirement. Solid planning that leaves flexibility for changes can make you or break you. Inflation, market fluctuations, unstable investments, expensive health care, long-term care, inflation, tax changes and the state of the economy as well as longevity are all significant factors to account for when structuring your retirement plan. Not planning for eventualities will lead to income shortfall.

Your success in retirement will depend on your own involvement as well as that of the advisor you choose to work with. Choose someone who is well-versed in the distribution phase of retirement.

Chapter 2:
Capitalizing on
Retirement Income Planning

Retirement is like a long vacation in Las Vegas.
The goal is to enjoy it the fullest,
but not so fully that you run out of money.
~JONATHAN CLEMENTS

To point out the obvious, once you stop working you're going to need to replace your paycheck. The main goal of "income" planning is to transition your capital into monthly "income" that you can count on to sustain the lifestyle that you want for the rest of your life.

Sounds easy, right? Not so fast! To have a successful outcome—one that will meet your needs through many years of retirement—you will need to have an Income Distribution Plan designed, constructed and implemented. If you possess the financial knowledge and experience, you can certainly do this yourself. If you don't, this should be done through a series of strategy sessions with a financial advisor who is experienced in income distribution planning.

Important Points to Consider

There are many considerations that you and your financial advisor should discuss in order to determine the right strategies for your retirement distribution phase. Once in place, your plan should be monitored on an ongoing basis, with an annual review conducted. This should occur even more often if there are life-changing events.

Risk Tolerance

One of the things you will need to analyze is your risk tolerance—not only how much risk would be prudent for your particular situation, but your personal tolerance level.

Be very careful whom you ask for advice. Risk tolerance is a very personal issue. You simply cannot do something just because someone else is doing it. Your situation is unique to you.

Believe it or not:

**YOU CAN TAKE LESS RISK AND
STILL DO VERY WELL IN RETIREMENT!**

A *retirement* income plan should be designed and constructed to be safe and secure with low risk and low volatility.

Social Security

There are strategies for getting the most out of Social Security that many people have never even heard about. Not doing this correctly could potentially cost you tens of thousands of dollars.

*** IMPORTANT NOTE ***

When I design a retirement plan for my clients, every single one includes a 22-page personal analysis report on their particular options which is based on their Social Security numbers. This report is GOLD! I do not know how anyone can design a plan without this. If your options are not clearly defined, someone is quite possibly costing you tens of thousands of dollars and it's likely that you won't even know it. You need to make sure a report like this is done for you. Be adamant about it. If you're told to do anything without being shown an analysis of your Social Security calculations, get a new advisor and don't look back.

Other Factors

You'll need to analyze life expectancy, inflation (for cost-of-living adjustments), and pension options. If you're one of the lucky few who have a pension, you will need to consider your spouse's income in the event that you die first.

You'll need to consider big-ticket items like new cars and vacation expenses. Take into account 401k rollovers, Roth IRA conversions, required minimum distributions, life insurance (a great tax planning strategy), medical expenses, long-term care expenses. The odds are that someone (you or your spouse) is going to need long-term care, so you need to plan for it.

You'll want to incorporate tax-reduction strategies. There are some excellent strategies you can use that may reduce your tax bill. You'll want to know what they are and determine if they are pertinent to your situation.

You'll want to do some basic (or not-so-basic) estate planning and legacy planning for your heirs if that's on your list.

Your plan should include well-thought-out strategies for income distribution, taking into account how that income will adjust for inflation and how it will be taxed, as well as how it is affected by poor market performance.

(One of many examples with regard to income strategies would be laddering, which is a method of bucketing your portfolio into different time frames or segments. Setting "laddered" maturity dates for consistent payouts offers you the ability to be conservative about immediate income and more aggressive for continued growth on dollars needed in the future. This is a great way to help ensure that you have consistent cash flow during your retirement.)

This is a good list to start with to help you begin to correctly assemble a retirement income plan that lasts for you.

All of this can be arduous to coordinate on your own. But it is certainly possible to do a great job on your own if you have the knowledge. For most of us, it is a better choice to enlist the help of a qualified retirement income advisor.

I once thought to save some money by fixing my own car. Instead of hiring an auto mechanic, I decided to replace the blown engine in my 1971 Cutlass. Needless to say, after I did in fact get the engine out of the car, I had no idea how to get a new one in and make it work. I did finally hire someone with the expertise to do the job. In the end, it cost me thousands more than it had to.

I have plenty of these stories. I'm sure we all do. There are times in life when it's best to consult experts, and your retirement income is crucial enough to warrant doing so.

For more detailed information on finding a qualified financial advisor, there are checklists and key questions in my companion *Retirement Planning Made Easy* workbook, which is designed to help you gather, sort out and apply all of the material cited throughout this book.

A Few Financial Questions to Get You Started

One of the main problems with retirement income planning is that the person retiring often doesn't know what needs to be accomplished. Because they don't have a grasp on what needs to be accomplished, they don't know what to *ask* to make the right decisions concerning their income distribution plan.

Here are a list of questions that you can use to assess how much you know about the process.

- Do you know how long your money would last if you had to stop working today, invest your savings, and live as safely as possible, while attempting to maintain your current living standards?

- Do you know of any Social Security strategies that will maximize the lifetime benefit for you and your spouse?

- Do you know how to build a retirement portfolio that is designed to create low risk and low volatility?

- Do you know how big of a nest egg you will need as you enter retirement, keeping in mind that you might be retired for 20, 30 even 40 years?

- Do you know the appropriate spending rate from your nest egg, so that your savings can and will last for the rest of your life?

- Do you know what percentage of your pre-retirement income you will need to replace to maintain your current standard of living in retirement?

- Do you know how the rising cost of health care could impact and potentially decimate your retirement income plan?

- Do you know what your pension annuity is worth and what it costs to buy more lifetime income?

- Do you know how longevity affects the way you structure your funding?

- If you have a retirement shortfall, do you know how big it is and what can be done about it?

- Do you understand the proper way to leave a financial legacy to heirs, including the most tax-*efficient methods?*

- Taking all of this into account, do you know if your retirement income plan is sustainable?

There are other things to consider, but this list represents the most critical points.

These questions will help familiarize you with the work that needs to be done in your portfolio. If you answered "no" to or are confused by any of these questions, you are not alone! The good news is that there are many solutions available for you.

Once you have taken a look at these questions to get your priorities in order, there are many ways to solve the "knowledge and strategy gap" that you may have discovered. Remember, most people are not successfully prepared for retirement. Going over these questions will help you better prepare.

Monitoring Your Progress

One of the most crucial mistakes retirees make is that they don't have their portfolio consistently monitored. In addition to ongoing monitoring of performance and stability, life-altering events may necessitate that your portfolio to be re-assessed and sometimes even re-designed. Life is full of changes and your portfolio will need to change with it.

If you feel that this monitoring is too much for you, or you feel you lack the expertise to do it, or you simply would prefer not to, there is nothing wrong with honestly admitting this. Partnering with a competent financial advisor for the management and maintenance of your portfolio (as well as its design and implementation) is a prudent choice. Your financial team will flag issues or report potential improvements to you periodically over time.

Monitoring your retirement portfolio will allow you to take advantage of key opportunities as well as avoid any potential risks, so that you can continue to enjoy your life and remain financially "worry-free."

The Recap

- **How much risk are you willing to take? Why or why not?** What will you do if you lose half your money? Research ideas that can help to keep you out of harm's way. Utilize strategies that help protect you from those losses so that you can continue to move forward. You don't need to be the person who spends years pushing the rock back up the hill just to get back to where you started.

- **There are many key considerations to determine strategies that will work specifically for the goals you have set.** Analyze life expectancy, inflation, pension options, big-ticket items, Social Security, 401(k) rollovers, self-directed IRAs, ROTH IRA conversions, required minimum distributions, life insurance, medical expenses, long-term care expenses, taxes, estate planning, legacy planning, income distribution strategies, and more.

- **Formulate the right financial questions now** so that you don't miss anything during the planning and designing phases. Write an outline first. By knowing the right questions and discussing them with a financial advisor, you can streamline your plan to suit your lifestyle, avoid risk, and capitalize on opportunities during your retirement.

- **A competent financial advisor should conduct a series of strategy sessions with you** to fully understand your goals. This is a critical step. YOUR plan cannot be designed properly if the advisor hasn't taken the time to ask all the important questions about who you are, what you want to accomplish, and where you want to end up. The advisor should also analyze your particular Social Security scenario and base recommendations on this individualized assessment.

- **Always monitor your progress,** and consider partnering with a financial advisor who will monitor your portfolio in a consistent manner. Your advisor should keep you abreast of any opportunities that come along or risks that need to be managed, in a timely manner, while maintaining the integrity of your retirement capital at all times.

Chapter 3:
Can You Afford To Retire?

"Before you speak, listen. Before you write, think.
Before you spend, earn. Before you invest, investigate.
Before you criticize, wait. Before you pray, forgive.
Before you quit, try. Before you retire, save. Before you die, give."
- WILLIAM A. WARD

You might be surprised at the number of people who are realizing that they can't afford to retire. I've lost count of how many times I've seen people in this unbearable position. That doesn't mean you are one of them, however, and there are some things that you can do to get an idea of where you stand financially with regard to this question.

Establishing Your Retirement Income Needs

Establishing whether you can afford to retire isn't as difficult as you might think. It can be a process, however, involving a number of moving parts.

In my opinion, it is generally a good idea to be conservative when factoring the income you think you'll be able to generate, and liberal when calculating your anticipated expenses.

Do you base your decision on how much you'll need—or do you base your decision on how much you have? That depends, and begs another question: Do you have time yet before you retire, or are you at the threshold?

Either way, you need to start somewhere. So start with calculating:

- what you anticipate your expenses to be

- what you know your fixed income will be, and

- an accurate list of your assets.

Expenses are going to be a best guess initially. There are many opinions on how to calculate. Some suggest anywhere from 50 to 100 percent of your current expenses. I've also heard a rule called "the 25 times" rule: in this scenario, theoretically if you have 25 times your annual expenses you'll be okay if you're drawing 4% a year.

There are probably as many different ideas as there are advisors. I prefer to be as accurate as possible based on the information I am given.

So, here's a basic approach to expense assessment: Make a complete list of what your expenses are going to be. Some things never go away. Food, electric, housing, insurance (auto, homeowners, life insurance, long-term care insurance, taxes (property tax, income tax), gasoline. These days most of us also need to factor in services such as Internet, cable and cell phones.

Expenses that people often forget include medication, Medicare expenses, supplemental plans, co-pays, entertainment, travel, clothing, gifts, personal items, even postage.

You can also probably think of others that are personal to you.

You also need to add a monthly dollar amount for unforeseen expenses.

When you have a number, now add a cost-of-living adjustment to that. For my clients I use 3% per year. Some years will be more and some years will be less; this serves as an average.

Now that you have that number, add up all of your guaranteed fixed income.

PENSIONS

Do you have any pensions? This does not include IRAs or 401(k)s. If you have different pension options, know what they are.

Many pensions give you different monthly income options to choose from. Each option comes with a cost. As an example, you may choose what's called a "maximum option" which means that you will get the highest payout available to you—but if you pre-decease your spouse, then your spouse gets nothing. Alternatively, you may choose another option in which your monthly payout will be less, but guarantees your spouse the same payment should you pre-decease him/her. Yet another option which may be available is a 50% option, where your spouse would receive 50% of whatever your monthly payout is.

These are some examples of what will likely be available to you. Generally, the more income that you secure for your spouse through your pension after you're gone, the less your monthly income will be.

If you are healthy and can afford to do so, you can "insure" your ability to take the maximum income available to you by purchasing a life insurance policy. If you should pre-decease your spouse, the pension would end, but your spouse would receive the proceeds from the life insurance policy income-tax-free. The proceeds should then be used to set up a monthly income to replace the pension lost at your death. The size of the life insurance policy would depend on the size of the pension. Should your spouse pre-decease you, you have the ability to cash in the life insurance policy for its cash value and continue receiving your highest pension payout. If you are not insurable, or you cannot afford to purchase a policy, you may have to choose an option that gives you less income, but insures that your spouse will continue to receive a payout from your pension.

Some people receive a pension statement every year that highlights their income options and the estimated amount they will receive. If you don't get one of these, this can be researched by going directly to the human recources department at your place of employment.

Once you have documentation on your options and corresponding payouts, assuming that you are insurable, an experienced financial advisor who specializes in retirement income planning can help you design a life insurance policy to suit your needs.

SOCIAL SECURITY

At what age will you begin collecting Social Security? Do you know what your best strategy is for this? This is an integral part of your plan. There are little-known caveats to claiming Social Security that can increase your income from Social Security substantially. An analysis can calculate those options for you, demonstrating different claiming strategies, indicating the monetary value of each, and suggesting which strategy yields the best outcome for your personal situation. You can also receive a plan of action for how to go about setting up that strategy. For some people, this can mean the difference of tens of thousands of dollars.

For some people, the decision to claim Social Security retirement benefits early may be the right choice—for example, if you don't have a long life expectancy, or you have no other income or no spouse. But for other people, the opportunity to receive a higher monthly income should not be overlooked. Strategies such as "file and suspend" and/or "spousal benefit" should be investigated. For more information you can go to **www.dmarra.sswise.com** (and also see **Chapter 9** of this book).

SAVINGS

Now we get to savings: IRAs, 401(k)s and any other investments you may have. Add up all your assets.

When you do this, you need two columns. One is for funds not yet taxed such as IRAs, 401(k)s, and qualified and non-qualified annuities.

(Interest is deferred on non-qualified annuities.) Since you haven't paid the "tariff" on this money yet, it isn't all yours. State and federal taxes will substantially reduce these monies. (Later on down the road—not too far!—you will want to consider specific tax strategies.)

The second column is for all other money. That would include savings, CDs, hard asset values, and brokerage accounts. If you plan on using any equity in real estate you can add that in as well, bearing in mind that you still need a place to live. However, perhaps you're thinking of selling your home and downsizing, leaving additional dollars to add to the pot.

I should also mention the cash value of your life insurance contracts. You have the ability to use the cash value for income, or to cash it out for a lump sum. Whether the cash value of your life insurance goes in the "all other money" column or the "funds not yet taxed" column depends on whether you will be cancelling the contract or keeping it in force and simply using the cash value for income.

If you cash the contract in (I don't recommend this at all) there will be tax due on any amount that you receive over and above what you have already put in. You will also be giving up the death benefit. The better alternative is to keep the contract in force and simply "borrow" the cash value out in the form of a loan. Loans are not taxable, although loan interest must be paid. Whatever you borrow will come off your death benefit when you die.

If you have a life insurance contract with a significant amount of cash value, you can call your insurance company and ask them to prepare an "in force life insurance proposal." Explain that you would like to turn the cash value into an income stream and you would like them to project that within the proposal, and also have the contract pay the loan interest. This will show you how long the contract can sustain itself based on its current and future (guaranteed) value. An advisor who is experienced in retirement income planning can do this for you. An advisor can also run an analysis to compare your current contract to newer, more innovative contracts on the market today.

If you are thinking about cashing in, this money belongs in the "funds not yet taxed" column. Calculate your cost basis (the dollar amount you put in the contract since you purchased it) and then calculate your tax liability on the remainder. (Tax must be paid in the year that you receive the money.) If you are going to borrow the cash value, then you can put this asset in the "all other money" column.

OTHER INCOME

Do you have any non-guaranteed income such as rental income?

Set aside a dollar amount from these assets for an emergency fund. This is an account that you *will not* be including in your withdrawal calculations. It can be invested and growing; it doesn't have to be in a 0% savings account. But you don't want to be invading your core portfolio for emergencies or you'll generate less income.

Now you should have an idea of what your annual expenses are. You should know what your guaranteed fixed income is and you should know the total of your assets, both tax-deferred and non-tax-deferred. (Separating these classes of assets will become important when you are tax planning and deciding on the best income source.)

Here is an example of what you will want to do with this information. Let's say that:

      Annual expenses are: $74,000 (1st year)
      Fixed income is: $47,000

Subtract your fixed income from your anticipated annual expenses and there is a deficit or gap of $27,000.

Now you know that you need to generate an additional paycheck of $27,000 (in the first year; inflation kicks in beginning year 2) from your investments.

Do you have enough to retire?

What Can You Do If You Fall Short?

The first thing you *don't* do is panic. If there is one thing I have learned in 30-plus years in this field is that if there's a will, there's a way. All is not lost yet!

If you are trying to retire "early" and the numbers aren't working out—well, nice try. Don't feel bad; most people can't retire early.

First, make sure that all of your calculations have been done correctly. I am not just talking about adding them up. Sometimes you can draw income from certain areas or at specific times that will help you to increase your front years (years 1 through 5) while allowing years 6 through 10 and years 11 through 16 (and so on)to grow to acceptable levels safely. I'll talk more about that later.

Ideas that you may want to consider:

If you are still a few years away from your desired date, consider increasing your savings. Small sacrifices today can go a long way in retirement.

- *Delay retirement.* Continue to work for a few more years. This will allow you to continue saving, as well as allow your assets to continue to grow before you start taking withdrawals.

- *Consider cutting back your hours if possible.* Half a loaf is better than none. You can be "semi-retired." Perhaps here you may be able to draw on Social Security (look at your analysis, as mentioned above or in Chapter 9), or your spouse may be able to draw on the spousal benefit under Social Security to make up the difference from your scaled-back hours. You can still leave your assets to grow.

- *Consider downsizing.* You may own a big house with a big tax bill. Heat and electric generally cost more in a bigger home too. Two ideas related to this: you might consider selling your home while you're still working, or selling your home as soon as you retire.

This may be too much of a sacrifice for you. You'll have to decide. For some, this can make the difference.

- *Take a closer look at the expenses you decided on.* Perhaps there are areas where you can cut back.

- If moving to a new area that is less expensive than where you are now, make sure you base your expenses on the cost of living there. This could put you right where you need to be financially.

- If your children are still living with you and not contributing, maybe it's time! (I see this quite a bit.)

Outcome Orientation and Risk Management

Investors are more than ever seeking outcome-oriented solutions with a strong focus on their specific needs, such as income and wealth preservation.

Each of us has our own objectives and set of goals that we would like to accomplish. One couple reaching retirement may feel like their main goal is to provide an inheritance for their children when they die. Therefore, they may choose a lower standard of living in order to meet that goal. Another couple at retirement may decide that they want to travel the world and spend all of their assets over the next 20 years, not giving a second thought to what their children inherit.

Outcome-oriented investing can be defined as the process of investing after goals and objectives are established for a client. Outcome-oriented investment models are designed and managed to deliver solutions that help meet a client's objectives. Strategies focus not only on income but on principal growth, management of volatility, and prevention of loss.

Risk management is defined as the identification, assessment, and prioritization of risks, followed by coordinated and economical application of resources to minimize, monitor, and control the impact of unfortunate events (as well as to optimally capitalize on opportunities).

Risk management is perhaps the most critical component of retirement income planning. Many people have what a mentor of mine calls a "hope and a prayer portfolio" with no idea how and why it's invested the way it is. If you don't know the "how and the why" of your portfolio, you cannot manage its risks (or be sure that they are being managed).

There is more to risk management than asset allocation and diversification. A buy and hold strategy lends itself to high volatility. It keeps you in the game when you should have been out! And volatility to the downside for people in or near retirement can be devastating.

From 2000-2002, the stock market lost more than 40%. The Dow hit an (at the time) all-time high on Oct. 9, 2007, closing at 14,164.43; by March 5, 2009—a little under 18 months later—it had fallen more than 50% to 6,594.44. A $500,000 portfolio was then worth $250,000.

If you were affected by the 2007-2009 stock market drawdown, and you were taking 4% a year from a $500,000 portfolio to fill an income gap, you would after the fallout be getting just half that: $10,000. If your income needs had not changed, and you thus continued to withdraw $20,000, you would now be taking 8% per year of your portfolio.

To add more insult to injury, it's going to be very difficult to bring that portfolio back to where is once was, for a couple of reasons. First, it simply takes time to recover losses as substantial as 50%. Secondly, you're continuing to withdraw 8% because you need the income. How long can this portfolio last?

Any portfolio that experiences drawdowns this large was missing "risk management." There was no downside risk protection. This is a problem at any stage, but it's devastating for people in or near retirement.

In my opinion, *tactical* asset management is far superior to the "buy and hold asset allocation" model. Tactical asset management attempts to protect a portfolio from downside risk first. Tactical management's goal is to keep your money out of harm's way in bad times and grow your money when opportunity presents itself. With monitoring and flexibility, it has the ability to go "risk off" at a moment's notice. That is to say: it moves to a cash position and remains there until it is safe to do otherwise.

Ask yourself this: If you can have low risk and low volatility with a high probability of success, why would you do anything else? If you can reduce your downside risk from 50% to 5-10%, why wouldn't you? Rather than spending what could be years trying to make up huge losses you may never recover from, wouldn't it be easier to just let the dust settle and pick up where you left off? How many 40 or 50% drawdowns do you think you can survive before you're looking to be the caddy rather than the golfer?

That's risk management. That's what *tactical asset management* will do for you.

Risk Tolerance

Risk tolerance can be defined as the amount of risk (drawdown) that an investor is willing to take. If the risk of losing money keeps you up at night, then you probably have very little (if any) risk tolerance. If the fluctuation of an investment doesn't bother you, then you have greater risk tolerance.

You should have a good understanding of your ability to handle risk. It's important to know how much risk you can handle psychologically before making any decisions about how to invest your money.

But there is another question that should be answered: how much risk *should* you be taking? This will vary depending on your age, your income needs, your portfolio size, and your financial goals.

Risk Capacity

Risk capacity has to do with the amount of risk that you *must* take on in order to achieve your goals. This involves exploring timeframes and the income requirements within those timeframes.

Balancing risk with needs is not always easy. It takes some time and effort to assess your personal situation. Good judgment is important. At times, the amount of risk necessary to achieve a goal doesn't always align with your tolerance for risk and what makes you comfortable.

On the flip side, someone with a high level of risk tolerance may take on more risk than is prudent based on other criteria already mentioned, such as age, income needs, portfolio size, and financial goals. This is dangerous and can lead to portfolio devastation.

Spend as much time as is necessary in this area.

The Recap

There are some key points that you need to recall so that you can discuss them with your chosen financial provider. Here is a recap of this chapter.

- **When establishing your needs,** it's generally a good idea to be conservative when calculating the income you think you'll be able to generate, and liberal when calculating anticipated expenses.

- **Calculate your expenses** and guaranteed income, and add up all your assets. Break assets into two categories, qualified and non-qualified. Subtract your known fixed income from your expenses to arrive at your income deficit or gap (or surplus). The deficit is the dollar amount of the "paycheck" you'll need to generate from your assets.

- **If you have a retirement shortfall,** consider delaying retirement, increasing savings, downsizing, relocating, and/or reducing expenses. You may want to consider going into semi-retirement rather than full retirement initially. Don't forget to look at your Social Security options.

- **Risk management is perhaps the most critical component** of retirement income planning. A "buy and hold" strategy lends itself to high volatility. Tactical asset management attempts to protect a portfolio from downside risk *first*, keeping your money safe in bad times and growing it when opportunity presents itself.

- **It's important to know how much risk you can handle psychologically** before making any decisions about how to invest your money. It's equally important to consider how much risk you *should* be taking, regardless of how tolerant you are.

Chapter 4:
Strategy Sessions

"You've got to eat while you dream.
You've got to deliver on short-range commitments while
you develop a long-range strategy and vision and implement it.
Walking and chewing gum, if you will."
- Jack Welch

The Free Consultation

When approaching retirement and all of its risks and pitfalls, it makes sense to engage in a process that will produce results. I know that most of you reading this book have been offered a "free consultation" somewhere along the line. If you visit my own website, you will see that on any page, you can enter your contact information and request a consultation.

Is it free? Well, let me put it this way: I don't charge people to have an initial discussion. But there is a cost to the "free consultation" if it's all you ever do. The things you'll miss out on by not engaging in a *process* with strategy sessions will likely cost you more financially than you will ever know.

A free consultation *is* a great opportunity for you to find the right person to engage that process. It's a chance to sit belly to belly with someone so that you can assess their level of knowledge, their planning philosophies, and their ideas about how to accomplish your goals. It's also an opportunity for you to listen to ideas that perhaps you haven't heard before.

To make the best use of this time, you should have certain items with you. These include at least two prior years' tax returns, Social Security information, brokerage statements, annuity statements, life insurance statements, 401(k) statements, IRA statements and pension statements. You should also have a list of your expenses, and any anticipated large future purchases. If the advisor requested that you fill out a questionnaire of sorts prior to this meeting, it's to your benefit to spend 15 minutes and get this done. It's important to be proactive: this is about your future.

For me, the consultation is the perfect opportunity to engage with a prospective client about their philosophies, ideas and goals. Sometimes it's a perfect match. Other times it becomes an educational process that allows you to consider another perspective and decide how you feel about it. Yet other times, we may be too far apart.

An Example:

Assume I am meeting with a couple in their 60s who are getting ready to retire. They have spent most of their accumulation years invested in the stock market. They're not sure why, which is common. They've been through a number of market drawdowns over the years. Their portfolio was hit with a significant 50% drawdown in 2008.

But now it's 2015, and in that seven years they have all but forgotten the mental anguish those extreme losses caused. Their portfolio took years just to get back to even, but now they are "on top" again, making money and feeling euphoric. The idea of moving to a more conservative position is just out of the question in their mind, even ridiculous. "The market is doing great, I'm doing great," they insist.

I will explain to them that my first priority will always be to help protect them from those big losses and then, secondly, to continue to help grow their portfolio. They are older, no longer working, and need this money to generate income. To experience a scenario like 2008's loss during the next stock market drawdown would be catastrophic to their financial well-being. How many times can they push the rock back up the hill?

They hear me, yet greed won't allow them to make logical choices based on their situation. We are too far apart.

Assuming, however, that after talking we are close to agreement on where to begin, then this consultation is a great time to accomplish some significant fact-finding and ultimately lead us into a planning process that will produce results.

Solution-Driven Strategy Sessions for Designing Your Income Plan

One of the greatest and unprecedented challenges of our time is how to make money last over long retirements. If you plan correctly the first time, chances are very good that only some minor tweaking will be needed going forward.

1. *The Initial Strategy Session*: If you've had a productive consultation, it should serve as your first strategy session. It should consist of a series of questions and answers for the gathering of information. Your income needs must be discussed, as should any fixed income you will be able to count on. You should be educated on risk tolerance and yours should be determined.

   The advisor will need your statements to conduct a third-party comprehensive analysis of your current holdings. Your pension and Social Security statements are needed for an analysis that will determine your best claiming strategy and how this will fit in to your income stream.

The advisor will also need your tax returns in order to conduct tax planning strategies, as well as your life insurance and long-term care contracts if you have these protections in place.

2. ***Successive Strategy Sessions***: How many times you meet with an advisor will depend on how much work needs to be done. In my experience it can be as few as three, with as many as four or five initially.

These meetings should consist of a recap of the first session, followed by a discussion involving your current portfolio. In reviewing this analysis, you will want to have a clear understanding of its design, its pros and cons, its performance, its risk management characteristics and most importantly, how it lines up with your stated personal risk tolerance.

The discussion that follows this should cover how this portfolio fits into your retirement goals. You'll need to look at any changes that should be considered going forward.

Your Social Security claiming strategy, pension options and tax analysis should be reviewed, along with income/asset protection strategies. Finally, you should review an initial draft of your income plan.

This is in my opinion a fantastic meeting for you, because if it's done correctly, it turns something that can seem so abstract into a very clear and concise picture. It gives you the ability to envision your financial picture 25, 30 even 40 years into the future. If everything is calculated on a conservative basis, accounting for cost-of-living adjustments, liquidity and flexibility for tweaking in the future, you will have in your hands a kind of "map" that you should be able to follow with ease.

Conservative assumptions are important. If your portfolio ends up performing better than planned for, that's great—maybe you can take more vacations, play more golf, buy bigger presents, or even be more generous with giving. But, if you make assumptions that are not on the conservative side and you fall short, where will you be?

Make sure that you have input. Don't be intimidated. Make sure that all of your concerns have been addressed and that a solution has been put into place for each of those concerns. If you've read up to here, you should have a very good idea of what you want and need.

3. ***Implementation:*** Once you are comfortable with the projected outcomes and results, and have a razor-sharp understanding of what has been designed to achieve them, only then should you move forward and start the process of implementation. How long this takes will depend on how many moving parts there are.

If you are moving your assets to a new advisor who is better equipped to serve your current needs—which is often the case when retirement rolls around—your previous advisor *should* help you to make this transition as seamless as possible. Sadly, however, this would be the exception rather than the rule.

If a previous advisor is resistant to your moving on, remember: this is business. And it's *your* business. Don't allow anyone to make you feel bad or as if you're making a mistake after all the careful planning you've done. Don't second-guess yourself. If you feel guilty about taking a new direction, just remember that this is your life and your future, and it's your right to do whatever you feel is best for you.

Financial advisors have areas of expertise. This is true in any industry. No one advisor can be all things to all people. While no one likes to see clients move away, one hopes that professionals will act accordingly. Anyone with integrity will thank you for being a client and wish you well.

Why Strategy Sessions are Important

As I'm sure you know by now, the process of planning out your retirement encompasses a great deal more than investing your money and hoping for the best.

I have met with far too many prospective clients who have admitted to going to one financial seminar, saying "Well, it *sounded* good, so I went for a free consultation and invested my money." After reading this far, ask yourself : "Did that advisor have that client's best interests in mind?"

Retirement planning is far more than simply investing your money. In fact, in my opinion, it's premature to consider any investment before doing the work required to develop a plan.

To do the job right, it must be done over a series of meetings, even if in the end it's determined that the client has a great plan and should stay put. I am embarrassed for anyone in my industry who obtains clients this way. That is a salesperson, not an advisor. I don't have to ask a client how working with someone like that worked out; he or she is now sitting with me looking for help.

Strategy sessions also allow you to build relationships. They are extremely educational if approached correctly. Most people understand risk tolerance in a way they never did before after I perform a 90-second exercise with them, and they know exactly where they stand. I'm not a genius; it's not difficult! It *is* a matter of taking the time to educate and investigate.

These are the key differences between a plan designed specifically for you, and one that is cookie-cutter. Retirement planning is not one-size-fits-all. It's deeply personal, and each design should be built to fit the needs and desires of the individual. This takes time, patience and understanding on both sides.

Have a General Outline Before You Begin

A general outline is a preliminary map and guidance tool. It gives you a place to start and an idea of where you want to end up.

Imagine that a friend of yours tells you about a vacation spot that he loved. He tells you the name of the place and what it looks like but that's it. Do you now get in your car and just start driving until you hopefully recognize this place? It's more likely that you will take the time to sit down, gather more information, and draw yourself a map. (This, of course, is assuming a GPS is not available) This way, you are far more likely to reach your destination.

You probably know what you want your retirement to look like. You've had years to think about it: what you want to do, where you want to live, vacations you want to take, volunteering you want to do. You may have also thought about the obstacles that might arise, and the money you think you'll need.

Write it all down—everything—including a wish list. Maybe you can achieve it all, maybe not. Write it down anyway. It's a place to begin.

(My companion *Retirement Planning Made Easy* workbook can help you organize and coordinate your written answers to these questions all in one place.)

Now your advisor will have a better idea of what you want your retirement to look like and what you want to accomplish. It will help to be on the same page right from the beginning.

Gather Relevant Information

Gathering the relevant financial information, as discussed earlier, is another key to preparing for the first strategy session. Here it is in check-list form:

- At least two prior years' tax returns

- Social Security statements (www.ssa.gov)

- Brokerage statements

- Annuity and life insurance contracts

- 401(k), IRA and pension statements

- Estate planning documents

- Beneficiary designations

- Existing debt information

- Information on real estate owned

- Preliminary budget information (expenses, anticipated purchases)

- Hard asset values

- Completed questionnaire, if requested

- A list of questions you would like answers to

Having these items will help the process to move along smoothly, and can ease unnecessary stress.

My companion *Retirement Planning Made Easy* workbook will prompt you to to gather and document everything you need, probe deeply into the right questions, and help you keep the information organized in one place.

The Recap

- **Is a "free consultation" really free?** Yes, but limiting yourself to just a no-cost conversation can cost you dearly if you don't engage in strategy sessions with an advisor. The free consultation is a great opportunity for you to check out an advisor and possibly hear new ideas. You'll likely know early on if you'd like this meeting to go past 30 minutes.

- **If you've had a productive first consultation, it can serve as your first strategy session.** It should consist of a series of questions and answers, along with gathering of information. Have all the necessary documents available. Be open-minded to new ideas and ask questions.

- **Successive strategy sessions** should consist of a recap of your last meeting plus discussion of any analysis that has been completed, and proposed ideas for your consideration.

- **Having a general outline before you begin** will give you a place to start and an idea of where you want to end up. It will also keep you on track and focused.

- **Gather the relevant information you need before the meeting.** Refer to the list in this chapter.

Chapter 5:
Building Your Plan With a Purpose

"A goal without a plan is just a wish."
ANTOINE DE SAINT-EXUPÉRY

"Productivity is never an accident. It is always the result of a commitment to excellence, intelligent planning, and focused effort."
PAUL J. MEYER

The Hope and a Prayer Portfolio

A great majority of people have what I would call "a hope and a prayer" portfolio. They *hope* that it does well; they *pray* that it will; but they have absolutely no idea why it should.

Modern Portfolio Theory—asset allocation, or "diversify, diversify, diversify"—is often touted as the key to all investing. In my opinion, it is not.

Taking the 2008 stock market crash as an example: did you have "asset allocation" that wasn't actively adjusted? Were you diversified? If so, did your portfolio suffer? It's very likely that it did, and it's also very likely that it was painful. And when it was all over, you had to push the rock back up the hill just to get back to where you were before it fell. It no doubt took a long time—if you ever got it back there—and was exhausting.

I favor instead (and suggest you consider) an investing style called "tactical asset management." This is a dynamic investment strategy that actively adjusts a portfolio's asset allocation. The goal of the strategy is to improve the risk-adjusted returns of passive management investing. The bottom line is that it is an *active* investment style rather than a *passive* investment style.

This is important: Your plan and portfolio MUST be able to go to a "risk off" cash position so that you are *minimizing* maximum drawdowns (losses) in your portfolio. That is what tactical investment management does. Can you imagine where you would be if your portfolio hadn't incurred the losses that most did in 2008 alone?

If You Don't Control Your Money, Your Money Will Control You

You've heard the expression "cash is king"? Well, even more to the point, *cash flow* is king. You can have one or two or three million dollars saved, but if you don't have a good, well-calculated, solid and proven system in place to disburse that money, usually one of two things happen:

1. **You spend money at a rate that far exceeds your limitations, because you haven't taken the time to understand what those limitations are.** Before you know it, you're in trouble. To *most* people, a million dollars is a lot of money. It's treated like an endless pit.

   Now, maybe you're thinking "not me, I'm not careless with my money, I would never do that,"—and hopefully, you're right. But most people have never had a million dollars sitting in their hands. It can be a very dangerous situation. Do you have any idea what it takes to be sure that money lasts the rest of your life, and the life of your spouse or significant others?

You could partake in the industry standard idea of withdrawing 4 to 5% per year. That's fine. It will work—unless, of course, you lose half of your portfolio during a market drawdown because you were inappropriately invested for distribution. Now you'll have to take 8% or 10% of that portfolio just to get the same paycheck—or continue to take 4-5% and live on a lot less.

2. **The other extreme is that you're so overly cautious that you're afraid to touch a nickel.** This attitude presents its own set of problems—the biggest of which is allowing fear to guide you. I have met with people so frozen by their fear of running out of money that they wouldn't allow themselves to reap the rewards of all their years of hard work and sacrifice. This is sad.

If you end up in either of these scenarios, your money is controlling you. I have witnessed both extremes more times than I can count over the years. It's not pleasant to be in either situation.

There is a third way, of course—and that is *balance*.

While I was raising my children—and I'm sure if you raised children, you'll understand this—there were times when they weren't doing well in some area of their lives. More often than not, it was school. A report card would come home and as I read it, I could see that their grades had suffered, falling beneath what they themselves had proven to be capable of.

I would explain to them that they had lost balance in their lives. I told them, "You cannot be hanging out with your friends all day and expect to do well in school. You need some time for studying, some time practicing your sports or your musical instruments, and some time for your friends. If you spend *all* your time with your friends and no time on the other things, then the other things will suffer."

With money, you need to find a way to balance spending too much with not spending any at all. You cannot frivolously spend and you cannot hoard money out of fear; either way some area of your life will undoubtedly suffer.

You need to create a plan and roadmap that will create that balance for you. If it's done well, it will act as a "permission slip" to live comfortably, within your means and without worry. That set of instructions will be your income plan blueprint.

A Blueprint for Long-Term Success

When we talk about building a retirement *income* plan, it isn't enough to just invest your money and let it ride. It isn't enough to decide on a particular style of investing and let *that* ride either.

Your plan needs a purpose. Where are you going? Where do you want to go? What is it that you want to achieve? Do you have the resources to get there and if not, what's the best that you can do with what you do have?

You need goals that are in line with your portfolio size so that they are achievable. As I mentioned in a previous chapter, you may have to adapt your goals and expectations.

You have a much higher probability of long-term success if you have a "strong probability" blueprint. That's a strategy with a central objective of reliable, inflation-adjusted income that lasts through retirement. If you continue to place the bulk of importance on **R**eturn **O**n **I**nvestment rather than on **R**eliability **O**f **I**ncome, you'll be putting yourself and your family in a completely unnecessary, high-risk position. Return on Investment simply is not the critical "ROI" when it comes to retirement.

The most efficient method we can use for this strategy gives you a 20- to 30-year forward view of your retirement. I will discuss this in terms of a 25-year forward view, since the majority retire at age 65 and looking ahead 25 years brings you to age 90. I will also cover the years beyond age 90, for those of us lucky enough to get that long of a run.

This strategy sets up six segments, each of the first five segments representing five years. These segments are designed to generate a reliable monthly income for the first 25 years, with a cost-of-living increase every five years. (It is certainly possible to attempt to provide a cost-of-living increase more often; however; to do so requires more assets or a higher rate of return.)

The amount of assets allocated to each segment will become progressively smaller as we move out in time. The further out a segment is, the more aggressive the investment can be. Still, *tactical asset management* as discussed will remain extremely important, employing measures at all times to minimize drawdown within all segments.

Segment #1 will be the most conservative, since you will be using this to generate your monthly income in the first five years. Once five years have passed, you move on to segment #2, which has already been invested for five years; then segment #3 which has now been invested for 10 years. This continues until you have reached the end of the 25th year.

Remember that we have set up for a sixth segment. This investment has been quietly waiting for 25 years. Assuming you made it this far, congratulations—you are now 90 years old! The goal of Segment #6 is to provide additional income should you live beyond 25 years, and/or to leave an inheritance to your heirs.

You can also consider one additional segment for anticipated or unanticipated large purchases.

For more information and education on this strategy, you can go to my website **www.marrafinancialgroup.com.** At the bottom of the home page you will see a section called "Helpful Resources." There you can click on the link "Retirement Time" and be taken to a detailed explanation, including video with real-life examples.

This method achieves a set of basic goals, as follows:

- You receive a reliable monthly income.

- This income increases with inflation over time.

- You maintain an amount of money (Segment 6) that can be used to generate additional income beginning in year 26, or that can passed on to your heirs.

- Liquidity remains an important factor, with the recognition that there is always a potential for unforeseen changes in financial circumstances.

While the further-out segments (which will be invested for longer periods) would seek to accomplish a higher rate of return over time, you would still be wise to consider investments that have the potential to significantly minimize your drawdown (or downside) risk. This is possible through tactical asset management.

The amount of money that should be allocated to each segment will depend on what age you retire, how much you have, how much income you need, your already-established income floor, the rate of inflation you use, among other factors.

In all of your calculations I would suggest that you remain conservative in what rate of return you expect. If you anticipate a particular investment to return 7% over time on average and you perform your calculations at a lower rate, you will be much safer. If it works even at a lower rate, then you have a better chance of success.

Evaluate this strategy in the context of your own personal retirement needs. I believe it will offer you the best opportunity to provide the retirement security you are seeking.

The Recap

- **Steer clear of a "hope and a prayer" portfolio.** Put serious consideration into tactical asset management—a dynamic investment strategy that actively adjusts a portfolio's asset allocation—and seek out investments that use this management style. Avoid passive asset allocation and those that lack balance; they bring with them far too much downside risk.

- **Cash flow is king.** Don't allow your money to control you. With money, you need to find a way to balance spending too much with not spending any at all. Develop an income plan that acts as your blueprint and it will allow you the freedom to live comfortably without worry.

- **If you are looking for long-term success,** take a long-term view. Be conservative in your calculations and plan for contingencies. Create a "strong probability" blueprint that sets you up for security.

- In retirement income planning, emphasize **R**eliability **O**f **I**ncome rather than **R**eturn **O**n **I**nvestment or you'll be putting yourself and your family at risk. Retirement brings the need for a different kind of ROI.

- **You can have your own blueprint designed** by clicking on "Strategy Sessions" at http://www.marrafinancialgroup.com

Chapter 6:
401(k) and IRA Rollovers

"Financial literacy is an issue that should command our attention because many Americans are not adequately organizing finances for their education, healthcare and retirement."
—RON LEWIS

What is a Qualified Plan?

A "qualified" plan is a retirement plan that qualifies for four tax benefits when it meets all of the requirements of Internal Revenue Code as well as the Employee Retirement Income Security Act of 1974.

Those four benefits are:

1. Employers can deduct allowable contributions in the year they have made contributions on your behalf.

2. You, the participant, can exclude contributions and earnings from your taxable income until you withdraw.

3. Earnings on the funds held by the plan's trust are not taxed to that trust.

4. Usually, you and subsequently your beneficiaries can continue to delay taxation of these funds by transferring them to another tax-deferred arrangement, such as an IRA.

Qualified retirement plans fall into three general categories:

1. **A defined benefit plan**: this is a "traditional" company pension plan where the retirement benefit is definite—either as a specified dollar amount or a percentage of your wages.

2. **A defined contribution plan**: the contribution to the plan is defined, but the benefit paid is not. The amount paid will be determined by how much is contributed and the performance of the investment. These plans can be government-sponsored or employer-sponsored as well as personal plans.

3. **Cash balance and other hybrid plans**: these offer elements of both defined benefit and defined contribution plans.

That's a very brief overview. There is plenty of in-depth information available on qualified retirement plans that explains rules, procedures, advantages and disadvantages. In fact, **irs.gov** is an excellent resource for more in-depth information on these plans; there are numerous publications on the subject.

If you have a qualified retirement plan, it will likely fall into one of these categories and further information on your particular plan is readily available to you.

401(k) plans and IRAs and are among the most common defined contribution plans. This chapter will focus on the rollover of the 401(k) and IRA.

401(k) and IRA, Defined

Just to make sure the terms are defined for you:

A 401(k) is a traditional, employer-sponsored retirement plan that is outlined in IRS tax code section 401(k)—hence the name 401(k). It's generally offered by an employer to its employees as a way to save money on a "pre-tax" basis. This means that your money is invested *before* tax and grows on a tax-deferred basis. The tax is not paid until you begin withdrawing from the account.

Once you begin taking withdrawals, every dollar is taxable at your then-current tax rate (both state and federal).

Participation in a 401(k) is not mandatory. Once you leave your job, whether you retire or change jobs, you have the ability to *roll* your money over to what's called an Individual Retirement Account (IRA). When you do this, you are simply moving your money away from the company's voluntary retirement plan to your own personal retirement account.

An Individual Retirement Account (IRA) is an account that you set up on an individual basis, rather than through an employer. The money you deposit is tax-deductible and the earnings are tax-deferred. When you later begin withdrawing money, every dollar is taxable at your then-current tax rate.

A Roth IRA is a type of Individual Retirement Account. The difference between the Roth IRA and a traditional IRA mentioned above is that when you put money in a Roth IRA, you are depositing that money on an "*after*-tax" basis rather than *pre*-tax. This means that you can *not* use the deposit as a tax deduction on your tax return.

Why would you want to do that? Because the Roth IRA is a "tax-free" account, meaning when you do begin taking withdrawals, every dollar is completely free from taxation at both the federal and state level.

Another difference between a Roth IRA and a traditional IRA is that with a Roth IRA, you never have to take distributions. You can pass the entire account on to your heirs, at which point tax-free distributions will begin. With a traditional IRA, you *must* begin withdrawals (required minimum distributions, or RMDs) at age 70 ½ or face some very heavy penalties.

To figure out your traditional IRA's required minimum distributions at a given age, you can use worksheets provided at **www.irs.gov**.

Rollovers

A rollover is simply the act of taking a distribution from one retirement plan—whether it's a 401(k) or an IRA (among other tax-qualified plans), and moving it into a new plan. It is an exception to the rule of taxable distributions; while being moved, the funds will not be taxed until a future taxable distribution, as long as certain rules are met.

That's where the simplicity of its definition begins and ends. There is actually quite a bit to know about doing a rollover properly so that you have a successful outcome.

Rollover Procedures

There are a number of procedures available to you when you are ready to proceed with a rollover.

Indirect (60-Day) Rollover: when you're taking a distribution—either partial or full—from your current qualified plan, the distribution is sent to you directly. To complete the rollover, you must deposit the funds into the new retirement plan within 60 days of the date that the funds were paid to you from the distributing plan.

If this is done correctly, the rollover won't be subject to tax. If you don't complete the transaction, or miss the 60-day deadline, the distribution becomes a taxable event, both on the federal and state level, and the amount distributed will have to go on your tax return as income for the year it was distributed.

If you are under the age of 59-½, you will also be subject to a 10% penalty for early withdrawal.

Your employer is obligated to withhold 20% for taxes. As an example, if you are taking a distribution of $100,000, a check would be issued to you for $80,000. You are still responsible for depositing the entire $100,000 in the new plan within the 60-day window. This means that you will have to come up with the other $20,000 from your other funds. You'll be able to recover the 20%, or the $20,000 that was withheld, when you file your tax return for that year.

If you miss the 60-day deadline, the IRS *may* waive the 60-day rollover requirement if the circumstances were beyond your control. There is a list of automatic waivers that can be found at irs.gov. In addition, there are procedures in place for you to request a waiver based on your particular circumstances. This can become a nightmare, so it is advised that you simply stay within the 60-day window and you won't have any problems.

The new account should be set up to receive your money prior to the actual rollover. Your new trustee will report this deposit to the IRS on IRS form 5498. You'll get a copy of the 5498. It's advisable that you keep this with your tax return information and receipts for the year the rollover took place.

Trustee-to-Trustee Transfer: also referred to as a direct rollover with employer retirement plans, this procedure moves your money from your current trustee (the account in which your money is being held) to a new trustee (where your money is going). You never receive the funds. The trustee has powers of administration of your money and a legal obligation to administer it for the purpose specified. This type of transfer has the least potential for error. The money is moving directly from one tax-deferred account to another so there is no potential for any tax consequences. It also eliminates the danger of missing the 60-day deadline. This is the safest, most efficient way to move retirement funds.

Remember, a check made out *to the new trustee for your benefit* is not subject to withholding. A check made out to *you directly* is.

It's fine to roll money over from your qualified plan to a personal IRA, but if you intend to move that money to your next employer's qualified plan, then *do not* comingle those funds with a previously funded IRA. Once you do that, you may lose the ability to move those funds back into an employer-sponsored retirement plan.

Instead, if you intend to move fund to another employer's plan, set up a separate rollover IRA into which to move your funds from your qualified plan.

There are pros and cons to moving money back to a qualified retirement plan with an employer. With a qualified retirement plan you are extremely limited in your investment choices. You may only choose an investment that is offered through that plan. With an IRA, your choices are vast. However, generally you may take a loan from a 401(k), while you cannot take one from an IRA (if you do, it is considered a taxable distribution).

Beneficiary / Inherited IRAs

So many mistakes are made with inherited IRAs (Beneficiary IRAs) that I will briefly mention some important highlights.

I have met with numerous individuals over the years who had inherited IRAs from people in their lives. By the time I met with them, they still had not taken a distribution from the inherited plan. Reasons varied from "I didn't know I had to" to "my accountant didn't tell me to" and even "my accountant told me I didn't have to."

This is a very costly mistake, as the penalty for not taking a distribution from an inherited IRA is 50% in addition to federal and state taxes.

Either a spouse or someone other than a spouse can inherit IRAs and 401(k) s. The rules are different in each situation.

When someone dies and leaves an IRA or any other qualified plan behind (like a 401(k)) they usually have either named a spouse as a beneficiary, or a "non-spouse" beneficiary.

As a spouse beneficiary, you have options:

1. You can treat the IRA as your own by designating yourself as the account owner.

2. You can treat the IRA as your own by rolling it over into your own IRA.

3. You can treat yourself as a beneficiary rather than treating the IRA as your own.

If you treat the IRA as your own, you have to follow the rules of a "normal IRA"—that is, you cannot take distributions until age 59-½ without a 10% penalty; you must begin distributions by age 70-½; and you can make contributions to the IRA. This is called a spousal rollover, and all normal IRA rules will apply. There is no deadline for completing spousal rollover.

If you treat yourself as a beneficiary, you *must* follow the IRS rules for inherited IRAs. You must open an "inherited IRA account" (also called "beneficiary IRA"). The money cannot be co-mingled with any other funds. Then you must begin taking distributions no later than a year after the death of the account owner. And those distributions will be based on the *beneficiary's* age, not the deceased owner's age.

You cannot make any contributions to this IRA.

(This language may sound confusing, so allow me to clarify: you have inherited an IRA, but even though you have inherited it, it is still essentially just an IRA. You must do the paperwork to actually create something *officially called* (you guessed it!) an *inherited IRA*—a special instrument for tax purposes into which you will roll the account you inherited. (Spouses can treat the IRA as their own by designating themselves the account owner, but everyone else must roll the account into an inherited IRA or take an entire distribution and pay the tax.)

There is NO 60-day rollover rule for inherited IRAs. Once a check is issued to you, the money becomes a taxable event immediately. You will want to initiate a trustee-to-trustee transfer to avoid this.

There certainly are situations when a spouse might want to create a beneficiary IRA (treating themselves as beneficiary rather than spouse). As an example, if a spouse is not yet age 59-½ and expects to need income (say, a 38-year-old single parent), the best option is to treat yourself as a beneficiary and roll the money over into an inherited IRA. Then you get required distributions every year, as required under inherited IRA rules. The money is completely liquid, you can take more than the required distribution amount—you can even cash out the entire thing. If the IRA is taken as your own, none of this is available to you without penalty under normal IRA rules.

A *non*-spouse beneficiary does *not* have the option of rolling these inherited assets into their own existing IRA. The separate "inherited

IRA" *must* be established, and these assets cannot co-mingle with another inherited IRA or your own IRA. If more than one non-spouse beneficiary is named, a separate inherited IRA will need to be established for each beneficiary.

The inherited IRA must be titled properly. It must be titled in the decedent's name for the benefit of the beneficiary, or some variation such as "John Smith, deceased, for the benefit of Jane Smith." "John Smith, beneficiary Kenneth Jones" will also work.

There are mandatory required minimum distributions (RMD) for inherited IRAs. These will need to begin no later than the year after the death of the account owner. It's important to note that if the deceased account owner was required to take a distribution, but had not yet taken one, you are required to take that distribution for them.

It makes no difference what the beneficiary's age is—distributions must begin no later than the year after the death of the account owner. The amount of the distribution depends on the age of the beneficiary. A six-month old child's distribution will be quite a bit less than a 50-year-old adult's, because RMDs are calculated based on beneficiary's remaining life expectancy from the single-life table in IRS publication 590.

Distributions are not subject to the 10% penalty rule, since you are required to take them.

You can take distributions over your life expectancy. You can take a lump sum; using this option, you will pay income taxes on the entire distribution, so you will want to look at your income tax situation. Depending on your own income and the size of the inheritance, the lump sum may put you in a higher tax bracket.

The other option you have available is the "five-year rule," in which distributions must be completed by December 31st of the fifth year after the original owner died. This rule applies only when an IRA owner dies *before* the beginning date of his or her required distributions.

There are many other rules, regulations, restrictions, and deadlines that must be followed for a successful outcome with regard to inherited IRAs. They are beyond the scope of this brief description. These are merely important highlights, and further research and discussion with a qualified advisor is highly recommended. In the case of inherited IRAs, it's actually better to do nothing until you are clear about the ramifications.

Consider a Conversion To a Roth IRA

Consider the possibility of converting your pre-tax dollars to a Roth IRA. If it works for your particular situation, you can save tens of thousands of dollars over the life of your retirement—and beyond.

You can convert your eligible assets to a Roth IRA regardless of income or marital status. You'll pay income taxes on the amount that you convert, in the year that you make the conversion. As an example, if you decide to convert $100,000, that amount will go on your tax return as income for that year.

You'll need to consider whether you have enough money in a non-retirement account to pay the tax on any conversion. In addition, how much of the asset can you convert before it moves you into a higher tax bracket?

You may also consider converting your pre-tax asset over a period of years; however, each conversion amount will have its own five-year period under the five-year rule for conversions (explained below).

You are required to own a Roth IRA for five years in order to withdraw earnings tax-free during retirement. There are several things to consider avoiding being penalized by the five-year rule with Roth IRA withdrawals.

In order to withdraw your earnings from a Roth IRA tax- and penalty-free, you must you be over 59-½ years old and your *initial* contributions must also have been made to your Roth IRA five years before the date when you begin withdrawing funds. If you did not start contributing in your Roth IRA five years before your withdrawal, your earnings would not be considered a qualified distribution from your Roth IRA because of its violation of the five-year rule.

With regard to distributions, there are rules for contributions and there are rules for conversions; there are rules if you are under 59-½ or over 59-½; and there are rules for if you have met the requirements for the five-year rule and if you have not.

If you are not yet 59-½ you can withdraw *contributions* you made to your Roth IRA anytime, tax- and penalty-free. If you haven't met the requirements of the five-year rule, *earnings* may be subject to taxes and penalties. If you *have* met the requirements of the five-year rule, earnings may be subject to *penalties only*. In certain situations, you may be able to avoid taxes and penalties.

If you are 59-½ or older you can withdraw *contributions* you made to your Roth IRA anytime, tax- and penalty-free. If you haven't met the requirements of the five-year rule, *earnings* may be subject to *taxes*. If you have met the requirements of the five-year rule, earnings are free from *taxes*. The difference here is that since you are over 59-½ you are not subject to penalties, regardless of when you take a distribution.

Roth IRA owners are never required to take distributions. This is because the tax has already been paid on the principal and the earnings are not taxable, assuming you follow the rules. Your beneficiaries, however, will be required to take distributions.

It's important to note that if you are currently required to take a minimum distribution for your regular IRA in the year you convert, you must do so *before* converting to a Roth IRA.

IRA "One Rollover Per Year" Rule

Effective in 2015, you are only allowed one rollover in any 12-month period from an IRA. This limit aggregates all IRAs that you own. So if you own five IRAs, they are all treated as one for the purpose of applying this rule. You cannot make five individual rollovers.

This change won't affect your ability to transfer funds from one IRA trustee directly to another. The rule only applies to distributions where *you* receive a check from the trustee. It doesn't apply to transfers that go directly from one trustee to another. There is no limit on the number of such transfers that can be made each year. This is yet another reason that a trustee-to-trustee transfer is your safest course of action.

Net Unrealized Appreciation

If you own publicly-traded employer stock in your tax-deferred employee-sponsored retirement plan, assuming that the stock has appreciated in value, it is advisable to consider this, as it can be an extremely beneficial tax strategy.

Assume you have a 401(k) valued at $600,000, and $250,000 of that value is derived from company stock. You can roll over $350,000 to an IRA and transfer the $250,000 in stock to a brokerage account. By doing this, you will avoid paying ordinary income tax on the stock's "net unrealized appreciation"—the difference between the value of the stock at the time you purchased it and the value when you take the distribution. This way you will only pay ordinary income tax on the value at which you purchased the stock, and capital gains tax on the "profit."

Company stock rolled over to an IRA is taxed as ordinary income when it is distributed. If you own company stock in tax-deferred employee-sponsored retirement plan, you should consult a tax advisor for advice before you do anything.

None of what you have read here is meant to be legal or tax advice. I am not an attorney or an accountant. I work with accountants and attorneys for that reason. I have given you a brief rundown of common scenarios, but by no stretch is this conclusive. The transferring or rolling over of tax-qualified assets is a huge arena with many rules, regulations, timelines and restrictions that are constantly changing. There are many variables to consider. Mistakes can be very costly and there are few exceptions for take-backs.

My advice to you would be to take your time. Don't make any moves at all until you are clear that you have a fair understanding of all the pros and cons of what you are considering. Also, don't just blindly assume that whoever you are dealing with knows it all. In my opinion, no one can possibly have all the answers to all situations. This is just too broad a field and each situation is unique. I have tremendous respect for those who readily admit that they don't have all the answers if they don't. This is a clear sign of integrity.

The Recap

- **There are three main categories of qualified retirement plans:** defined benefit, defined contribution, and cash balance/other hybrid plans. It's likely that if you have a QRP you will fall into one of these categories. Once you have determined which you have, you can narrow down your research and educate yourself in that area.

- **Rollover procedures can include** direct rollovers (trustee-to-trustee transfers), and indirect (60-day) rollovers. Be sure you have a clear understanding of each and how each could benefit your particular situation.

- **Inherited / Beneficiary IRAs** do not have a 60-day rollover rule. Once a check is issued, it becomes a taxable event. There are different rules for spousal and non-spousal beneficiaries. You are required to take distributions, but have choices on how you will receive distributions.

- **A Roth IRA conversion** can be a great strategy depending on your situation. You can create tax-free retirement income for life that never hits your tax return. Understand how the five-year rules for contributions as well as conversion apply. If you are required to take a distribution, you must do so before the conversion. Once you have completed the conversion, you never have to take a distribution (though any beneficiaries do).

- **There is a "one rollover per year" rule beginning 2015,** extending over any 12-month period, so if you roll over money in June you must wait 365 days (until the next June) to do another rollover. It is advisable to do a trustee-to trustee transfer when moving your money. You can do as many as you like this way and you won't subject yourself to taxes and penalties. However, the one rollover per year applies to all IRAs, so if you have five, you can't treat them separately; you can still only do one per year.

- **NUA (Net Unrealized Appreciation) should be considered** if you own publicly-traded employer stock in your tax-deferred employee-sponsored retirement plan.

Chapter 7:
Basic Estate Planning Strategies

"I want to leave my children enough that they feel they can do anything, but not so much that they do nothing."
- WARREN BUFFET

An estate plan is a collection of legal documents that are prepared in advance of your incapacitation or death. These documents allow you to leave clear and concise instructions about your intentions when you are unable to do so. Once complete, it ensures that your assets as well as your healthcare are managed according to your wishes.

Estate planning tends to be one of the most critical parts of your retirement plan, and yet because of its unpleasant or uncomfortable nature, people often ignore it or leave it until it is too late. Virtually no one likes to think about their own death or incapacitation and what comes afterwards. There is a line in a song by Paul Simon: "I will continue to continue to pretend my life will never end…"

But taking the time to do this will make all the difference to your family and the legacy you leave behind. A good estate plan is the greatest gift you can leave your family when it's your time to go.

Experts call estate planning an "act of love" because it's not something that will directly benefit you; instead, it will benefit your loved ones. It can involve many complicated and heartfelt decisions, so it can be an emotional experience for you (and for your spouse, if you are married). It may help to view the process as being not so much about your death as about your deep care for your loved ones.

Why Do You Need An Estate Plan?

If you want control over who will handle your affairs should you become incapacitated, and over what happens to your assets when you're gone, you simply need to do something about it—sooner rather than later.

People who do nothing in this regard leave a mess for their families to clean up. I have witnessed this nightmare firsthand many times. It rarely goes well and it's completely avoidable. This is not the last memory that most people want to leave for their loved ones. I believe it is our responsibility to put a plan in place before these events happen.

You might be amazed at how many people think that they don't have an "estate." The fact is, even a child with a small savings account has an estate. Obviously, estates vary greatly in size and some require only simple documents to manage, while others necessitate a vast amount of planning.

A young single person may need only a beneficiary form for their 401(k) and life insurance, some form of power of attorney, and healthcare directives. Funeral arrangements or instructions are always helpful too.

By contrast, far more in-depth planning will be required to address the estate complexities of the married couple with a blended family, five children, nine grandchildren, a home or two and accumulated wealth.

You should use whatever strategies are available to you to help control how your estate is taxed, how it is managed, and of course how it is distributed. If you do nothing, your family will likely be paying taxes, court costs, and attorney fees they would not otherwise have had to pay. You will leave it to the courts to decide how your estate will be distributed—and that distribution may look nothing like what you would have wanted.

Do you want to give the government, the courts, and attorneys money that could easily have gone to your family? Do you want the courts telling your family who gets what? If you have small children, do you want the courts deciding who will become their guardian? I'm hard-pressed to believe this would be acceptable for most people. Yet by not placing a plan into effect, that's what you've set up.

Yes, it will cost some money to set up an estate plan. However, depending on the size of your estate, it may cost your family a lot more than the cost of an estate plan if you do nothing.

While cost is certainly a consideration, it's far more important to have a clear understanding of the proposed plan design and what it will accomplish. Interview several estate-planning attorneys. I would recommend favoring an attorney whose primary focus is on estate planning, and who has years of experience with this. It's very likely that you'll pay more for this, but once again, you do tend to get what you pay for.

Planning Your Estate: Your Part

To begin, you need to know whom you want to include and whom you want to exclude. Today, many families have divorces, multiple marriages, stepchildren, step-grandchildren and so on. You may or may not wish to include all members of a blended, extended family; that's up to you.

For example: you will probably want to include your children and grandchildren, but you may want to exclude their spouse(s). Or suppose your spouse remarries—do you want your estate to fall into the hands of the new partner (or his/her children) once your spouse is gone? There are ways to prevent these occurrences.

Think about the personalities and family dynamics you're dealing with. Some people are good at handling money; others are not. Some spend and some save. Is there someone who is great at managing money? Is there someone competent who is great at paying attention to detail and following your instructions? Maybe that's the person you should consider to be named as your executor (or trustee, for trusts).

Who may need stipulations on distributions? Do you have under-age children you want to provide for? Who will be the trustee of their inheritance? What about older beneficiaries, such as your parents? Do you feel they are able to handle an inheritance, or do you think they will need help? If so, from whom? Do you have any special charities that you would like to include?

Put an inventory list of assets together. Include: real estate and how it's titled; bank accounts; brokerage accounts; 401(k)s, IRAs, life insurance policies, hard assets, and so on. You'll want to list where the account is held, the account numbers, and beneficiaries. This would be a good time to check and confirm your beneficiary designations. Do any of the accounts have a TOD (transfer on death) or DUD (due upon death) naming beneficiaries?

Other assets that should be on your list include cars, boats, jewelry, artwork, collections, digital assets such as websites, and furniture, just to name a few. Are there specific people who you would like to receive these items? Write it down.

You should also list any liabilities that you have. Are there existing loans or other debt that will need to be settled?

Once you have a list included, preferred beneficiaries for your estate, and have prepared an inventory of your assets, decide who will get what. For some assets, such as IRAs and life insurance, you can use beneficiary forms. Other assets will need to be manually listed—this would be true of a vehicle or appliance, a jewelry or stamp collection, or a piece of art of furniture.

If you become incapacitated, who will make medical decisions for you? Will they have access to your medical records? Who will handle your financial affairs? Write this down. Make sure your selected individuals know who they are and what is involved.

You will need to make a decision regarding whom you will name as your executor. This is the person that will administer your estate when you're gone. These are enormous responsibilities, so choose wisely. Have a conversation with the people that you choose, and make sure they are comfortable handling these responsibilities for you. Have a contingency list in place as well, in case your first-choice executor is unable to perform these functions when the time comes.

Put together a list of contacts such as financial planners, bankers, life insurance agents, accountants and attorneys with whom you do business. Include their addresses and phone numbers.

Have you planned for funeral arrangements? Some people pay for their funeral in advance. It's another way of taking a load off your loved ones at a very difficult time. If you do this, your family needs to know about it. The arrangements may be the last thing they look for when you die, and if they aren't aware that you've already taken care of it, you may end up paying for your funeral twice. Make sure your wishes are written down and make sure your loved ones know where this information is kept.

In our current times, another important document to leave behind is a digital asset guide, including usernames and passwords to any online accounts or websites. Some online services keep all your passwords secure, so that the executor of your estate will have access. With these, only one username and password will be necessary to access all the others. Some people are very comfortable with these services, and others are not. This is a personal decision. But if you don't find *some* way to leave this information to your executor and loved ones (even if it's a typed-up list or piece of paper), accessing your files and accounts may be very troublesome indeed.

Finding Good Legal Advice

Are you updating an existing plan? If so, you may want to consider using the attorney that created it. Since he/she already has your information, and assuming you've already built a working relationship, it may only take a brief conversation over the phone or in person to facilitate any changes. This will save you the nuisance of telling your entire story again, and it will probably save you some money.

If, on the other hand, your financial and/or personal situation have had significant changes, or you feel you would benefit from a greater degree of sophistication, then by all means consider making a change. The most important thing is that you're buying the level of expertise that your situation warrants. Read on for a few ideas on finding a new attorney to suit your needs.

If this is the first time you're having an estate plan prepared, or you are in the market for a new attorney, the following are some steps that you can take to find one who is right for you:

- If you have an ongoing relationship with an accountant or a financial advisor, I assume you trust their judgment; this may be a good place to start. Ask this advisor for a referral to an attorney used by other clients with comparable circumstances.

- Perhaps you already know (and like) an attorney or two, but their expertise lies in other area of the law. They may be an excellent resource for you.

- Martindale.com is a well-known nationwide directory that allows you to search in your specific location as well as in a particular area of practice.

- The American College of Trust and Estate Council is another resource. According to their website, members are *elected t*o the college by demonstrating a high level of integrity, commitment to the profession, competence, and experience in the area of trusts and estates. Their website is actec.org.

Once you have narrowed your choices down to two or three, make the phone calls and set up the consultations. You may even be able to have the consultation via phone rather than face-to-face meeting. Personally, however, I would prefer to meet a prospective attorney face-to-face. Either way, this is your next step.

After you've made the decision about which one you will hire, gather everything you've put together and meet with your new attorney. He or she will conduct a fact-finding assessment, for which you will be completely prepared because you did your part (you might pleasantly surprise the attorney with your knowledge and preparation!).

Keep Your Plan Current

Estate planning is not something you do once and check off your to-do list. Life changes constantly, and some events are significant and affect your estate. Laws are always changing and evolving as well.

In general, to keep your estate plan current, having it reviewed at least once every three to five years is a good idea (and more often in the event of significant life changes). Here is a short list of events that may require you to update your plan:

- The birth of a child or grandchild
- The death of a spouse
- Death of a child or grandchild
- The sale or purchase of a home
- Serious illness
- Purchase of a business/sale of a business
- Significant increase or decrease in assets
- Change in marital status
- Death of other beneficiaries
- A move to a new state
- Relationship changes with beneficiaries or fiduciaries
- New tax laws
- New marriages
- Children reaching adult age

Basic Estate Planning Documents

There are several common estate-planning documents that you should be aware of. Understanding the purpose and function of each of these will prevent you from leaving out anything important, and will educate you on the range of potential options when formulating your plan.

- **Last Will and Testament**: This is the most basic estate-planning document. Its purpose is to state how your property will be distributed upon your death. Here you will name the recipients, or beneficiaries, of your property; an executor and contingent executor who will administer your estate; and who will take care of minor children. Those are the basics; other more advanced planning techniques can be included. For example, you can direct that trusts be set up for minor children.

- **Beneficiary Forms**: A document that allows you to specifically name the person(s) or charitable organization(s) to whom a particular asset will go upon your death. They are generally revocable, meaning you can change the beneficiary designation at will. An irrevocable beneficiary setup (less common) would need the actual beneficiary's consent to change. Accounts that have beneficiary designations pass outside probate. It is not necessary to place these accounts inside a trust. Such accounts can include savings accounts, CDs, IRAs and other tax-deferred accounts. Ensure that these forms are filled out and check them frequently for accuracy.

- **Power of Attorney (POA)**: There are different types of POAs that serve different needs. A **Limited POA** will give someone the power to act on your behalf for a limited purpose (e.g., if you need to sign a deed and you are not available to do so. A **General POA** is much more comprehensive. It gives your attorney-in-fact (person you designate) the same power that you yourself have—

for example, the power to sign documents and conduct financial transactions on your behalf. These may be rescinded, and end upon your incapacitation or death.

A Durable POA remains in effect even *after* you become incapacitated. Without this, if you do become incapacitated, no one can represent you in court unless and until a conservator or guardian is appointed by the court. These can also be rescinded prior to incapacitation and can remain in effect until your death.

A **Springing POA** allows your attorney-in-fact to act for you *if* you become incapacitated and does not become effective until you *are* incapacitated. It is important to indicate the standard for determining incapacity that will trigger the POA within the document.

- **Healthcare Power Of Attorney** (also called health care proxy): In this document, you can authorize someone you trust to be your health care agent to make medical decisions for you when you are unable to make them for yourself.

- **Living Will**: This is also known as your *advanced medical directive*, a *patient advocate designation*, or an *advanced directive*. This document spells out how you should be cared for in an emergency when you cannot speak for yourself or you are incapacitated for any other reason. It covers topics such as desired quality of life and end-of-life treatments, including treatments you do not want. It also covers resuscitation. It provides a way to "speak" with the doctor who is caring for you when you cannot, and advises him/her about how to approach your care and treatment. You should be as specific as possible within this document about your wishes.

- **Trusts:** Trusts are a massive and intricate subject about which entire books are written; they are beyond the scope of this book.

The most common type of trust which you have likely heard about is a *revocable living trust*. Depending on your circumstances, a revocable living trust may or may not be helpful. The more assets you have, the more helpful a trust can become. Assets that already have named beneficiaries, however, do not need to be titled inside a trust.

- **Inventory of Assets**: A comprehensive list of all your assets, as mentioned previously in this chapter. This should be done prior to meeting with an attorney. You do not need an attorney for this.

- **Personal List of Contacts:** This details who your personal advisors have been: attorneys, bankers, accountants, financial advisors, etc. Include your utility and service providers too. You will save your family hours and days of frustration by documenting this information. You don't need an attorney for this.

- **Digital Asset List:** This list should contain usernames and passwords for your digital assets, such as websites or online properties, credit card accounts, and any other account that you think your executor may need to access. You don't need an attorney for this.

- **A Document Detailing Your Funeral Arrangements**. You can state your desire to be buried or cremated, along with any other express wishes. This should also be discussed with your family or the person(s) who will take care of your burial prior to your death. It's possible that they won't read or be aware of this document until it's too late. You do not need an attorney for this.

The above list is enough to get you started; it may be all you need. Never assume that your own estate is too small to require your attention. Larger estates will require more advanced planning. It is always to your advantage to meet with an attorney who has the knowledge and expertise in estate planning. They are trained to recognize potential problems you may know nothing about.

The goal should be to have your estate administered in a timely fashion with few to no issues along the way, passing on a legacy to your loved ones that you can be proud of.

We are all going to die someday. What degree of planning you need is obviously going to be based on your personal situation.

Don't procrastinate—just dig in and get it done. Get a check-up every few years or so and feel good that you've done the best that you can do to make a difficult time easier on your loved ones. Just follow the simple steps I've laid out for you in this chapter. A few hours later you'll be ready to put your plan into action. Get your part done and leave all the technical stuff to the professionals. Let them earn your money and your trust. It will be worth every penny and more.

The Recap

- **Estate Planning** offers you the opportunity to help control how your estate is taxed, how it is managed, and how it distributed. Take advantage of everything that is available to you. Professional expertise can reveal opportunities you may not be aware of that can save you and your family money and hassle. If you don't learn about these, you may give the government, courts, and attorneys money that could have gone to your loved ones.

- **Remember** that this is not so much about your death as it is about your love for your family or treasured companions. You'll make a hard time easier for them if you plan now, and that's a gift. Leaving a mess behind for our loved ones is not the legacy most of us wish to be remembered for, but it's what happens if you procrastinate or avoid this planning. Not having your wishes carried out regarding finances or your own medical care is also a real risk of not planning.

- **No estate is too small to have a plan for;** never assume your estate doesn't warrant a plan. Younger people may have less to arrange than older people with larger families and financial complexities, but everyone has an estate.

- **Prepare a list of the people** you would like to include as beneficiaries to your estate.

- **Prepare an inventory of your assets.** Decide who will get what and when you would like them to receive it.

- **Decide who will handle** your medical care decisions and your financial affairs should you become incapacitated, and who will administer your estate when you're gone.

- **Other important things** to cover are a list of contacts, documented funeral arrangements, and a digital asset list.

- **Hire an estate-planning attorney** and have your plan prepared. Remember to keep it current: have your plan reviewed every three to five years, as well as after any life-changing events.

Chapter 8:
Annuities

I advise you to go on living solely to enrage those who are paying your annuity. It is the only pleasure I have left.
- VOLTAIRE

Americans should consider putting as much as half of their assets in an income annuity.
- GOVERNMENT ACCOUNTABILITY OFFICE

Imagine for moment that you are purchasing a lottery ticket. When you're filling out the form, you have a choice as to whether you want your winnings in a lump sum, or in equal payments over a specified period of time.

When you choose equal payments over your lifetime, you are choosing an "annuity" option. The payments are guaranteed.

How about Social Security? You pay in taxes throughout your working years and at some point, when you retire, you are paid a monthly income that you cannot outlive. These payments are also guaranteed.

Then there are pension plans such as "defined benefit" plans. Again, once you retire, these pay you a monthly income that you cannot outlive. These payments, too, are guaranteed.

The payout model that all these income sources are using is an *annuity* concept. It's noteworthy that some of the most dependable, well-known sources of income to which nearly everyone in America will be a beneficiary use the annuity model as their underlying structure.

Annuities have received some pretty bad press over the years. Perhaps it's time people started to take note of exactly where that information is coming from. Could it be the know-it-all (however well-intentioned) neighbor or brother-in-law, who heard it from someone else at a BBQ, who read half an article that they really didn't understand? Could it be the mechanic who is excellent at repairing cars—and also knows everything there is to know about annuities because he heard it from a friend who heard it from a friend?

Could it be an advisor who doesn't sell annuities? Or an article writer who heard about annuities for the first time this morning and decided it would be a good topic to write about?

In my 32 years in this field, I have *never* seen one person say *no* to a pension or Social Security check. People count on these sources of income. Why? Because they *can* count on them. It may be the only thing that they really can count on.

You most certainly cannot count on the stock market, for example. As I write this, we have been in a 6.5-year bull market. Suppose now that you are in the home stretch of your working years and you're invested in the stock market. What will you do if tomorrow is the day that this bull market turns around and drops, 30, 40, 50%—as it has so many times before?

If you had even a portion of your money in a particular kind of annuity, that money would still be there, ready to dole out your next monthly check like the unwavering soldier. Your stock market money? Well, if you're taking the classic 5% a year, be prepared to take 5% of a lot less.

As I hope is crystal clear by now, retirement *income* planning isn't about getting rich. It's about assurances that no matter what happens, you always have the resources to generate the income that you'll need to continue to live the lifestyle you wish. Never lose sight of that, or you may someday find yourself in a financial disaster that you cannot recover from.

What Is An Annuity?

An annuity is a product—a financial instrument that is offered by life insurance companies. Annuities are referred to as *contracts* or *policies*.

You deposit your money in an annuity through an insurance company. The insurance company makes certain contractual guarantees, as well as rules for taking money out. Each annuity has a specific "term," or timeframe during which your money must remain invested if you want to avoid incurring a "surrender charge."

All annuities can be "annuitized," which means you give up all rights to the principal (e.g., it must remain with the company permanently) in exchange for guaranteed income for a specified period of time. The other way to get a guaranteed income is with an income rider, which lets you take income payments and still eventually get the lump sum back if you want. (Of course, once you take the principal out, you no longer have the income.)

If you haven't annuitized but want to withdraw money from the contract value before your term is up, and that withdrawal amount is over the 10-15% allowable annual withdrawal privelege, you will pay a surrender fee on the overage. The surrender charge schedule is based on a descending percentage (meaning the sooner you take it out, the more of a charge you will pay). A withdrawal made prior to age 59-½ may be subject to a 10% federal tax penalty. This goes for both qualified and non-qualified money.

The interest earned on an annuity is tax-deferred until withdrawal. And withdrawals from annuities are taxed based on what's known as a "last in, first out (LIFO)" model.

How does this work? You deposit your money (principal) in the annuity. Then, interest is earned over the next year and added to your principal. Since the interest was "last in," it will be the first to come out.

The interest will then become taxable and you will receive a 1099 for the year you made the withdrawal.

You will never be taxed on the principal in an annuity unless of course it is IRA money (you can put an IRA into an annuity), in which case principal and interest *are* taxable, no matter what investment vehicle you use.

Most annuity contracts have a 10% annual right of withdrawal (some are higher, such as 15%, but most are 10%). This means that the insurance company allows you to withdraw up to 10% (or 15% or whatever the right of withdrawal) without having to pay the surrender charge described above, even before the term of investment is complete. Only if you go over the stipulated percentage would you pay a penalty on the overage.

You may also take required minimum distributions surrender-charge free, even if they are larger than the "right of withdrawal" percentage. At age at 70-½, if your annuity was purchased with IRA money, you will have to take required minimum distributions, and this protects you from paying a penalty even if the RMD is larger than the 10% (or whatever it is) your right of withdrawal allows you to take during the annuity's term.

If you die before the annuity's term is complete, the balance will go to your beneficiary surrender-charge free regardless of their age, and no 10% federal penalty will be imposed upon the beneficiary.

You may also "annuitize" the contract and begin taking income. If you annuitize the contract, again, you essentially have given up all rights to the lump sum of money and the insurance company's obligation to you becomes monthly payments based on an option you choose. A few of examples of those options are lifetime payments, life with the remainder to beneficiaries, a 10-year certain payment (payments made for 10 years), or a 20-year certain payment.

Annuities are designed for growth and safety. They have the ability to guarantee a stream of income for life that you cannot outlive. They are also tax-deferred investments. This is a huge benefit, because the money inside the annuity has the ability to grow at a faster rate.

In addition, if you are collecting Social Security, this arrangement has the potential to save you thousands of dollars in taxes that you might otherwise have paid on that Social Security income. This has to do with the "provisional income calculation" that is done when you are preparing your tax return. There is an IRS formula for this.

Different Types of Annuities

There are a number of different types of annuities. Which one fits your particular situation will depend on your personal needs.

Immediate Annuity: These are purchased with a lump sum of money. This is a product that is "annuitized" within the first year, often immediately after purchasing it. Payments commence generally within the first year. When you purchase an immediate annuity, you give up your right to the money in exchange for a monthly benefit based on the amount of years you have chosen to be paid. While some don't like giving up access to their money in this manner, the income can often be greater and more secure than those that give you more access. It's a good idea to compare.

You can start annuities in advance of retirement or once into retirement, putting any portion of your assets into the product. (In one concept, the **advanced-life deferred annuity** (ALDA), someone in later retirement—often aged 80-85—may invest a small percentage of their assets into an annuity, to help ensure income for a longer period should they live past the capabilities of their majority investments.)

Fixed Deferred Annuity: These are generally purchased with a lump sum of money. You can also make additional payments. They pay a fixed, specified rate of return that is declared at the beginning of the contract. They are deferred from taxation until withdrawal. Interest is earned annually and remains within the contract (until withdrawal). At some point, when you choose, you can begin taking income. Or once the surrender years have passed (remember that annuities have a surrender period during which you are charged a fee for withdrawals that are over the free "right of withdrawal" percentage), you can withdraw the entire cash value of the contract. You will then pay tax on the interest. There is no tax on the principal (the money that you deposited)—unless the money you deposited was qualified money (i.e., an IRA), in which case both the principal and the interest are taxable when withdrawn. You do not have to annuitize these contracts at any time.

Fixed Index Annuities: These are generally purchased with a lump sum of money; however, many allow future payments. The interest crediting method (how interest is earned and credited to your annuity) is different from the fixed annuity, however. There are also many different combinations, far too many for the scope of this book. There are a number of good books written on the subject of fixed indexed annuities that you can read. One such book is *Stress-Free Retirement* by Patrick Kelly. The interest earned is tied to one or more stock indexes. This offers you potential for a greater rate of return. The most widely used index is the S&P 500. It's important to understand that your money is not invested in the stock market; rather, the potential interest that you can earn is based on how the index performs, and based on your contract specifications, you are credited a certain percentage of that gain. If the stock market goes down, you do not lose any of your accumulated money—you simply earn a 0% return that year. Your principal, and any interest already earned, is protected from loss and guaranteed. You essentially get upside potential with no downside risk. Fixed indexed annuities are also tax-deferred and when you decide to take a withdrawal, only the interest earned is taxable—unless of course, it is an IRA.

Variable Annuities (VA): Variable annuities are classified as a security product, and as such have a prospectus (a legal document which is filed with the Securities and Exchange Commission that provides details about an investment offering for sale to the public). You should request one and you should read it. It will contain everything you need to know.

You can purchase an immediate or deferred VA. With the immediate VA, you will take income immediately; with the deferred, you'll defer income for a specified period. They are both tax-deferred and work in the same manner as a fixed annuity.

Unlike fixed and fixed indexed annuities, when you invest in a VA it's important to understand that your money *is* invested in the stock market. If the stock market goes down, you will take a loss on your principal and interest earned. While there are a few low-cost VAs out there, even those carry the risk of the stock market.

The majority of VAs on the market have administrative charges that can run anywhere from 0.10% to 0.50% per year, and you'll also pay a "mortality expense" at an average of 1.35% per year, according to Morningstar. Other fees such as expense ratios, transaction costs, and sales charges average approximately 3.1% per year, according to Forbes. All these fees can add up to as high as 4.7% per year. You will need to do better than your fees for your money to grow. In good times, you can. In bad times, however, VAs will generally parallel the stock market. There are also surrender charges.

VAs are a high-risk option for someone preparing for retirement, and in my opinion the fees associated with them far outweigh the benefits. Most do have a fixed interest account. My thought is: why pay all the fees if you're going to put your money in a fixed account? Just purchase a fixed annuity if you're going to purchase anything at all.

Transferring Between Annuities

You can also transfer one annuity to another. This is called a 1035 exchange. Over time your situation may change so that another type of annuity complements your needs better than the one you have. New products are constantly being developed and approved for the marketplace. By moving your money via a 1035 exchange, the money continues to maintain its tax-deferred status and no tax will be due. If you do a 1035 exchange prior to the surrender period, that charge will be deducted from your account prior to transfer.

Guarantees for annuities are based on the claims-paying ability of the insurance company. Most states have insurance guaranty associations that are generally governed by a board of directors and the state's insurance regulator. Guarantees are for a specific dollar amount of your deposit; some are as high as $500,000 in the event that an insurance company fails. According to the FDIC, however, no insurance companies failed in 2009 after the 2008 stock market crash—while 140 banks closed their doors.

The Guaranteed Lifetime Income Benefit (GLIB) Rider

A GLIB rider can be added to an annuity to can guarantee a stream of income for life without having to annuitize the contract and give up rights to your principal.

When you deposit money in an annuity, every year going forward the company sends you a statement that shows the principal you deposited, plus any interest that was credited to the account. This is called your *surrender value*—the amount of money that you are able to withdraw at any time after a specified term is over (unless you annuitized and gave up rights to that money).

When an income rider is added to an annuity, it essentially creates a second value. This is called an *income value*. Your annual statement will also show this income value. You *cannot* withdraw this value and walk away with it like you can with your surrender value. The income value can *only* be received through income payments.

Why would someone add this to a contract, and what is the benefit?

For illustrative purposes, first let's go back to your surrender value, the money you can withdraw at anytime. Suppose you deposited $150,000 in the annuity and it earned a return of 5% over the next 15 years. At the end of the 15 years, assuming you didn't withdraw anything from the account and your surrender period was over, you would have accumulated $313,152. You could withdraw any amount of that money at any time you wish. (You can also allow it to keep accumulating.)

Then you have the income rider. Let's say that the insurance company guarantees to credit this income rider with 7% interest each year. The initial income value when the contract starts is based on the same amount that you deposited in the annuity—$150,000. After 15 years at 7%

rate of return, the income value would be $416,272. This is $103,120 higher then the actual surrender value. But remember, you do not get to walk away with this income value; it must be used for annual income payments.

In essence, your investment offers *either* a surrender value (which you can access and withdraw) or a higher value that is income value (that can *only* be used for income and not withdrawn).

Once you decide to begin an income stream from an income rider, the company will calculate your annual income based on the value of the rider, your age, and your gender. The income you receive will begin to reduce your surrender value. You will still have the option to withdraw that *surrender* value at any time.

If you choose to withdraw your surrender value—the $313,152 in this illustration—and cancel the annuity, you will forfeit the use of the income rider and its value. In fact, it will no longer exist.

This is one illustration of how an income rider could work. There are other methods used to credit interest to an income rider.

Income riders have a nominal fee attached. A typical fee could be between 0.5 to 1.5 percent. The fee is deducted annually from your accumulation value. If you know ahead of time that you will not be using the annuity for income but simply as an accumulation vehicle, then a rider may not be right for you.

Income riders are not offered with every annuity, but if they are offered, they are only offered at the time of purchase/setup. They cannot be added later.

The Recap

- Don't take everything you read and hear about annuities at face value. (Including what I have to say!) Apply your own due diligence as always. Remember, there are as many philosophies as there are advisors. Ultimately, you have to decide what works best for you and your personal situation. But if guaranteed income is on your retirement income wish list, placing at least a portion of your money into annuities can be an excellent choice.

- There are many different types of annuities. Understand the different types available to you and how one may benefit your situation over another. What particular segment of your retirement are you trying to cover with your annuity? That can be important to your choice.

- Remember that there is limited liquidity during "surrender years" (the specified term during which you don't have access to the principal), so you should maintain liquid accounts outside an annuity.

- You can transfer money inside an annuity from one company to another without a tax penalty by performing a "1035 exchange."

- Guarantees are always based on the claims-paying ability of an insurance company.

Chapter 9:
Social Security Planning

---

*We put those payroll contributions there so as to give the contributor
a legal, moral and political right to collect their pensions and their
unemployment benefits. With those taxes in there, no damn politician
can ever scrap my Social Security program."*
- FRANKLIN D. ROOSEVELT

A well-thought-out strategy for claiming Social Security benefits can result in substantial additional retirement income. So try to refrain from running down to the Social Security office and signing papers until you have the facts or until you have had a Social Security analysis done for you.

Social Security retirement benefits help provide lifetime, inflation-adjusted income. Coupled with your retirement savings and any pension benefits you might receive, Social Security can serve as an important element of your final plan for retirement income.

Important Definitions for this Chapter

Full Retirement Age

Full retirement age (FRA) is the age at which a person may first become entitled to full or unreduced Social Security benefits. If your birthday is on January 1, the previous year's FRA will determine your full retirement age.

Currently this ranges from 65 to 67 years of age, depending on your year of birth.

YEAR OF BIRTH	FULL RETIREMENT AGE
1943 through 1954	66
1955	66 and 2 months
1956	66 and 4 months
1957	66 and 6 months
1958	66 and 8 months
1959	66 and 10 months
1960 and later	67

Primary Insurance Amount (PIA)

This is the amount of monthly income you'll receive at your normal retirement age. Also known as **monthly benefit at full retirement age**.

You can find your monthly benefit at full retirement age on your annual Social Security statement or from the online statement.

Your PIA will be based on your lifetime earnings, and may be reduced according to when you decide to claim your retirement benefits. You can claim benefits as early as age 62, and you can delay them to age 70.

Modified Adjusted Gross Income

Modified adjusted gross income (MAGI) is generally defined as all of your taxable income, plus certain net foreign income, minus allowed deductions. MAGI may include income such as taxable pensions, wages, interest, dividends, and other taxable income plus tax-exempt interest income (such as interest on municipal bonds); and any exclusions from income, such as interest from U.S. savings bonds.

See Internal Revenue Code Section 86b(2) or Internal Revenue Service Publication 915 for more information.

Be sure to consider your retirement plan distributions. Generally, all distributions from IRAs and employer plans will be included in MAGI. Roth IRA distributions will not be included.

Effective Tax Rate

The effective income tax rate is the average rate at which income is taxed. It takes into account the deductions and credits used to compute income taxes. It is total income taxes divided by total income, and is less than the "tax bracket" or marginal rate.

Reductions For Retirement Before Full Retirement Age

You may start Social Security retirement benefits as early as age 62; however, each month you start prior to FRA will result in a reduction in your benefits. This reduction ranges from 25% for those with a FRA of 66, to 30% for FRA of 67.

Delaying Retirement After Full Retirement Age

If you choose to delay starting Social Security benefits, you will receive an increase in your benefit amount of 8% per year up to age 70. After age 70 there are no further credits for delaying benefits. The credit is two-thirds of 1% for each month beyond FRA.

As an example, if your FRA is 66, and you delay four years until you're 70, your monthly check will be 32% higher than at age 66, and 75% higher than at age 62. This can be significant.

Years ago, when age 65 was synonymous with retirement, the average life expectancy was 61.7 years. Perhaps it made sense to begin collecting a benefit at age 62. In 2012, the average life expectancy for females was 81.2 years; for males, it's 76.4 years.

To take this further, in 2010, a married couple age 65 had a 50% chance of one spouse living to age 92 and a one in four chance of one spouse living to age 97.

In addition, as of 2010, 5.8 million Social Security beneficiaries were at least age 85. These facts were taken from the Source Annuity Mortality Table from the Society of Actuaries.

Another interesting fact as quoted on my own Social Security website:

> The very first person to collect Social Security retirement benefits was named *Ida May Fuller.*
>
> A resident of Vermont, Ida May retired in 1939 after paying into Social Security for just three years. Ida May received her first Social Security payment on January 31, 1940. She then went on to collect from Social Security for thirty-five years. Ida May passed away in 1975... *at the age of one hundred.*

Given this data, I suggest that delaying Social Security—if you are in a position to do so—can be quite beneficial in terms of guaranteed income. You shouldn't assume that claiming benefits early is the best decision.

People tend to think that Social Security planning is as simple as figuring how many years it would take for them to break even if they collected early and picked up those four or so years. Nothing could be further from the truth. That is a very simplistic analysis, and it could end up costing you a significant amount of money over your retirement. Your retirement income plan should include a plan to maximize Social Security.

Strategies You Should Know About

File and Suspend

Social Security rules provide that a spouse, whether or not he/she has ever worked, is entitled to a benefit equal to up to one-half of the other spouse's retirement benefit. This is called a spousal benefit. You may even hear the term "free spouse" in reference to this benefit.

The spousal benefit can be initiated a number of different ways in different scenarios, such as for married couples, widows and divorcees. It also works out differently at different ages (for example, if spouse is at full retirement age when initiating vs spouse younger than FRA, so it's important to analyze timing and results carefully.

A spouse may not claim a spousal benefit unless and until the main beneficiary claims his/her benefit first. This doesn't mean that the main beneficiary *must* begin *taking* his/her Social Security benefits. It just means that he or she must *file* for them before the spouse can claim a spousal benefit. Once the main beneficiary *files*, the spouse may receive a percentage of those benefits whether the main beneficiary is receiving benefits or not.

In order to take advantage of this, there is a strategy called "file and suspend." This strategy can work very well for married couples. Once full retirement age is reached, a beneficiary can file for benefits, and then immediately suspend receipt of those benefits until a future date. Doing this allows his or her spouse to claim "spousal benefits" under the main beneficiary and receive one-half of the main beneficiary's benefit. The main beneficiary can then delay his or her benefit till age 70, letting that retirement benefit grow at 8 percent per year in delayed retirement credits.

For the spouse who is taking the spousal benefit, there is a significant difference between taking it *before* their own full retirement age and waiting until their own full retirement age.

If you take a spousal benefit *before* your full retirement age (such as at your minimum retirement age—you do have to be at least at minimum retirement age), you will be stuck with a lower benefit permanently.

As an example, suppose you claim the spousal benefit at age 62. Doing so could result in a spousal benefit as little as 32.5% of the main beneficiary's primary insurance amount (whereas waiting until you are full retirement age to file a restricted application and collect a spousal benefit would give you 50% of the main beneficiary's primary insurance amount).

Plus, if you are not already at full retirement age yourself, you will not be allowed to let your own retirement benefit continue to grow.

On the other hand, if you wait until your own full retirement age (let's say 66) and *then* began collecting the spousal benefit, you receive 50% of the main beneficiary's retirement benefit. *And* you are also delaying your own benefit to age 70—so it grows by 8% per year in delayed retirement credits.

If you take the spousal benefit, once you reach age 70, you would then switch over to your own benefit—assuming it is higher than the spousal benefit portion of the main beneficiary's benefit. If you don't have a benefit of your own—e.g., if you have never worked—you could continue to collect the spousal benefit.

By implementing this "file and suspend" strategy, the main beneficiary will have accomplished increasing his or her own monthly benefit by 32%—8% per year in delayed retirement benefits.

By taking the spousal benefit and delaying his or her own benefit, the spouse will *also* have accomplished increasing his or her own monthly benefit by 32%.

Both spouses are now getting 8%-a-year increases by not collecting benefits, and one spouse is collecting some benefit while they each allow their own benefits to grow by a total of 32% by the time they begin receiving full benefits. This is a perfectly legal way to receive some income while maximizing your ultimate Social Security benefits.

NOTE: It's very important when you file for the spousal benefit that you file a *restricted application*, so that you don't end up filing for your full benefits yet. If you don't file a *restricted* application, you would begin receiving your own fill benefit, not delaying it and receiving the spousal benefit.

IMPORTANT NOTE

POTENTIAL CHANGES TO FILE AND SUSPEND

A new bill has been proposed (at the time of this writing) that would significantly change the File and Suspend strategy with restricted application. If the bill is passed, which is likely, the proposed changes are as follows:

You would no longer be able to "file and suspend" for the purpose of triggering a benefit for your spouse. In order for a family member to claim a benefit on your Social Security record, you will have to be actually collecting your own benefit. With this change, there would be no benefits paid to anyone while your benefits are suspended.

*You **would** still be able to file and suspend to allow your own benefits to grow by 8% per year until you are age 70. That will not change. But a spouse could no longer claim spousal benefits during that time.*

If you attain the age of 62 by December 31st of 2015, you would retain your right to collect a spousal benefit at your full retirement age. Anyone who is younger than 62 on that date will not be eligible to collect a spousal benefit. If you are entitled to both a retirement benefit based on your own earnings record, AND a spousal benefit because you're married (or divorced after at least 10 years of marriage) to someone who is eligible for benefits, you could receive only one of these—the higher of the two amounts.

That said, there remain hundreds of different scenarios to be addressed, and laws are always changing, so Social Security planning must continue to be a cornerstone in your retirement income planning.

The Best-Kept Secret: Do-Overs

If you begin collecting Social Security and then change your mind, you may be able to withdraw your application. There are rules in place that allow for changes, including a 12-month window after filing in which you can repay all benefits you and your family have received. You can find the complete procedure at www.ssa.gov.

Divorcees: If you were married to the same individual for 10 years or more, you may be entitled to collect spousal and/or survivor benefits based on your ex-spouse's work history. You must be unmarried. Both you and your spouse must be at least 62 years of age, and you are not required to wait until your ex-spouse files for benefits. You must have been divorced for at least two years.

Widows/Widowers: You can begin receiving full benefits at FRA or reduced benefits as early as age 60. They can begin collecting benefits as early as age 50 if they are disabled started before or within 7 years of their spouse's death. If you remarry after age 60, it will not affect your eligibility for survivor benefits.

Single individuals: I'm afraid there is not much to add if you are single. You will collect under your own benefits. You should consider delaying Social Security benefits until at *least* full retirement age or even age 70 if possible. You most certainly can have an analysis done to show what your payments will be at various ages.

People with government pensions who worked for an employer that did not withhold FICA taxes from your salary, your pension may reduce your Social Security retirement benefits. This affects people who have a pension in a job where FICA taxes were not taken out of your salary but also work another job long enough to qualify for Social Security. This is called the Windfall Elimination Provision.

Based on the Government Pension Offset provision, if you will be receiving a pension from any federal, state or local government where you did not pay FICA taxes, your Social Security spousal benefit may be reduced. This doesn't start until you begin collecting your non-covered pension. You may want to consider waiting to begin taking your pension if you can collect at a later date and it actuarially increased.

Taxation of Social Security

About one out of three people who get Social Security have to pay income taxes on their benefits. Combined income is the sum of your modified adjusted gross income (see definitions earlier in chapter) plus nontaxable interest plus half of your Social Security benefits.

Per the IRS: A quick way to find out if any of your benefits may be taxable is to add one-half of your annual Social Security benefits to all your other annual income, including interest and dividends, taxable pensions, investment income, wages and tax-exempt interest. Next, compare this total to the base amounts below. If your *total* is more than the base amount for your filing status, then some of your benefits may be taxable.

The three base amounts are:

For single, head of household, qualifying widow or widower with a dependent child, OR married individuals filing separately who did not live with their spouses at any time during the year: If all your income added together (along with half your Social Security income) is between $25,000 and $34,000, then up to 50% of your Social Security income may be taxable. If all your income added together (along with half your Social Security income) is more than $34,000, up to 85% of your Social Security income may be taxable.

For married couples filing jointly: If all your income added together (along with half your Social Security income) is between $32,000 and $44,000, then 50% of your Social Security benefits may be taxable. If all your income added together (along with half your Social Security income) is more than $44,000, up to 85% of your Social Security benefits may be taxable.

For married persons filing separately who lived together at any time during the year, the base is $0.00—which means you will pay tax on 85% of your Social Security benefits if you have other income and use this filing status.

You may want to consult with an accountant. It is possible through sound financial planning and strategies to eliminate this tax burden even if you fall into one of these base income brackets.

This is a broad overview of Social Security benefit strategies. But it covers the main points about what you should be looking for, and more knowledge will add to your success in securing the absolute best Social Security claiming strategy possible.

All of this may seem complicated and cumbersome, but it needs to be understood if you want to give yourself the best chance for an optimal retirement income. Make sure that that whomever you are working with knows how to strategize Social Security.

You can also go to my business website at **marrafinancialgroup.com** and link over to my satellite Social Security educational website for further information, education and examples. In addition, I offer a Social Security Strategy session in which you will be able to obtain a complete 22- to 27-page Social Security analysis based on your own personal situation. This will point you to your best claiming strategy.

At the bottom of the home page you will see a section called "Helpful Resources." Click on "Social Security Wise" for more detailed information, including video with real-life examples.

What if you work during retirement?

You may work while receiving Social Security benefits, and working may mean higher future benefits. However, while working, your benefits may be reduced until you reach full retirement age. A formula determines the amount benefits will be reduced based on your age.

If you are under full retirement age for the entire year, benefits will be reduced $1 for every $2 earned above the limit. In the year you attain full retirement age, the deduction will be $1 for every $3 over $41,800 (2015). Starting with the month you reach full retirement age, there is no longer a reduction in benefits or a limit to the amount you may earn.

After full retirement age, the Social Security Administration will recalculate your benefits, considering the months when benefits were reduced or withheld due to excess earnings. In any year when earnings are higher than a prior year in your earnings record, the higher year will be used to recalculate your PIA and your payment amount.

If the Social Security Administration is notified in advance of your anticipated monthly earnings, they will adjust your payments accordingly.

If the Social Security Administration learns of the excess earnings later, they withhold all future payments until excess benefits are recovered.

The Recap

- **Social Security** benefits provide lifetime, inflation-adjusted income. It is a vital element in your retirement income planning and should not be taken lightly. It is no longer as simple as going down to the Social Security office and applying for benefits. Depending on your situation, there are specific strategies you can employ to make the most out of these benefits.

- **Key terms** to know are Primary Insurance Amount (PIA) and Full Retirement Age (FRA).

- **Key strategies** to consider are the "file and suspend" strategy that takes advantage of the spousal benefit, as well as divorcee and widow/widower strategies.

- **There are strategies** you may be able to implement in your income planning to reduce taxation of Social Security, even if you fall into a base income bracket that makes your Social Security benefits taxable. You'll need to consult with a competent tax accountant.

- **You can work during retirement and still receive Social Security,** but benefits may be reduced until you reach full retirement age. The earnings will be used to recalculate your benefits if they're higher than any year in your previous earnings record.

- **You can have your own Social Security analysis done** by clicking on "Strategy Sessions" at http://www.marrafinancialgroup. com.

Chapter 10:
Long-Term Care

*"I do believe we're all connected. I do believe in positive energy.
I do believe in the power of prayer. I do believe in putting good out into
the world. And I believe in taking care of each other."*
- HARVEY FIERSTEIN

Long-Term Care

Long-term care is a topic that few retirees want to talk about or even think about, and yet the potential need for it is a reality that many of our aging population must confront. With the risk of chronic diseases and illnesses increasing as we age, there is a good chance that during your retirement, you or your spouse will need some type of long-term care.

The notoriously steep expenses associated with long-term care can result in financial ruin if you do not plan ahead for it. I have seen people spend their entire savings to cover long-term care expenses.

In my experience, the main reason that most people don't have long-term care protection (insurance) is because they don't want to spend the money. But it is *far* more expensive to pay for long-term care on your own than it is to have secured some kind of protection (like a long-term care insurance policy) in the event that you need it.

Consider looking into the purchase of a long-term care policy. Shop around or have your advisor shop around for you to come up with a few ideas.

This type of coverage will protect your assets to the extent of the dollar value of the plan. As an example, a $200-a-day benefit for 365 days would protect you from having to spend $73,000 in that year. If a plan covers you for three years, that is $219,000. Double that and you have just protected $438,000 over a three year period.

Making a sound decision about whether to purchase long-term care insurance involves weighing the probabilities. You have to decide if it is worth it to you to pay the premiums for many years, even if you do not use them. When you purchase a homeowner's policy to protect your home, you probably do so because it gives you peace of mind that, in the unlikely event that your house burns down, it can be rebuilt and you won't be out on the street. It is a simple transfer of risk.

You have to decide if having protection in the event of a long-term care situation will give you peace of mind that your entire nest egg won't be wiped out to pay for your care at the end of your life.

You may be thinking "What if I never use it?' That's a reasonable question. Here's the answer: has your house ever burned down? For someone reading this, that may be a yes, but for most, it isn't. Did you still pay for homeowner's insurance? Are you glad you did?

Ultimately, the "right" decision will be evident only in hindsight. Your decision to purchase long-term care insurance or not is a personal choice that will revolve around things such as your health, your financial position and the health of your spouse.

An entire book could be written on this subject. My purpose in touching on it is at the very least to have you think about it—and consider how not insuring against a long-term care event could devastate you as well as your family.

Below are some facts from Morningstar.com that I think you might find interesting to review:

- **37 million**: Number of Americans age 65 or older in 2005.

- **81 million**: Expected number of Americans age 65 or older in 2050.

- **9 million**: The number of Americans over age 65 who needed long-term care in 2012.

- **12 million**: The number of Americans expected to need long-term care in 2020.

- **40%**: The percentage of the older population with long-term care needs who are poor or near-poor (income below 150% of the federal poverty level).

- **78%**: Percentage of the elderly in need of long-term care who receive that care from family members and friends.

- **34 million**: Number of caregivers who provide care to someone age 50 or over.

- **$113,640**: The maximum amount of assets a healthy spouse can retain in order for the other spouse to be eligible for long-term care benefits provided by Medicaid.

- **49%**: Percentage of nursing home costs covered by Medicaid in 2002.

- **25%**: Percentage of nursing home costs paid out of pocket in 2002.

- **7.5%**: Percentage of nursing home costs covered by private insurance in 2002.

- **79**: Average age upon admittance to a nursing home.

- **40%**: The percentage of individuals who reach age 65 who will enter a nursing home during their lifetimes.

- **892 days (2.44 years)**: Average length of stay for current nursing-home residents in 1999.

- **272 days (8.94 months)**: Average length of stay for discharged nursing-home residents in 1999.

- **38%**: Percentage of nursing home patients who will eventually be discharged to go home or to another setting.

- **10%**: The percentage of people who enter a nursing home who will stay there for five or more years.

- **65%**: The percentage of people who entered a nursing home who died within one year of admission.

- **Five months**: The typical length of nursing-home stay for patients who eventually died in the nursing home.

- **25%**: The percentage of deaths in the U.S. that occurred in nursing homes in 2010.

- **40%**: The expected percentage of deaths in the U.S. occurring in nursing homes by 2020.

- **68%**: The probability that an individual over age 65 will become cognitively impaired or unable to complete at least two "activities of daily living"—including dressing, bathing, or eating—over his or her lifetime.

- **42%**: The percentage of individuals in nursing homes who are experiencing some form of dementia.

- **33%**: The percentage of individuals in nursing homes who are suffering from some form of depression.

- **71%**: Percentage of patients with advanced dementia who died within six months of admission to a nursing home.

- **$73,000**: Median annual rate, nursing-home care in U.S.

- **3.63%**: Increase in median annual nursing-home costs since 2011.

- **4.5%**: Annualized increase in median annual nursing home costs, 2008-2012.

- **$162,425**: Annual cost of nursing home care, Manhattan, NY.

- **$60,773**: Annual cost of nursing home care, Des Moines, IA.

- **$86,140**: Annual cost of nursing home care, Tampa, FL.

- **$41,000**: Average annual base rate for residence in assisted living facility, 2012.

- **$20**: Average hourly rate for licensed, non-Medicare-certified home health aide.

- **7 to 9 million**: Estimated number of U.S. residents who had private long-term care insurance in 2010.

- **59**: Age of typical purchaser of long-term care insurance in 2010.

- **79%**: Percentage of long-term care insurance purchasers with more than $100,000 in liquid assets.

- **44%**: Percentage of population age 50 or older with more than $100,000 in liquid assets.

The Recap

- Almost no one wants to talk about or think about long-term care, but with our aging population living longer and the increased risk of chronic diseases as we age, it's a topic we must confront.

- Many people are inclined to gamble that "it won't happen to them" but statistics suggest that during your retirement, you or your spouse are very likely to need some kind of long-term care. It's a good idea to review the statistics and be familiar with the probabilities.

- Cost is the main reason most people don't obtain long-term care coverage, but it is *far* more costly to pay for long-term care out of pocket than with a long-term care insurance policy.

- For some reason, many people worry "What if I never use it?" regarding long-term care. Yet most people are glad they have homeowner's insurance in case the house burns down, even though for most people that will never happen. Having protection in the event of a long-term care situation offers the same peace of mind: your entire nest egg won't be decimated to pay for care at the end of your life.

Conclusion

You have reached the end of *Retirement Planning Made Easy* and I am confident that this information offers you an excellent foundation of knowledge to begin your own retirement portfolio-building journey. You now have a blueprint for planning a safer, more secure, low-risk retirement.

I urge you to find an advisor to work alongside you as you begin piecing together your retirement portfolio to secure your future. I also encourage you to use the companion *Retirement Planning Made Easy* workbook to help further support, guide, and structure your inquiries and information-gathering as you work with your advisor.

These are some of your most important years—the years where you kick back and enjoy the fruits of your lifelong labor, or perhaps engage in the creative expression or contributory volunteerism you always dreamed of giving your time to, once you stopped having to work.

You cannot do those things if you are constantly worried about money and security. I believe that a sound, secure retirement portfolio is one that is as predictable as possible. You win this race by going slow and steady. You can do very well in retirement with minimal risk.

Growing older does not mean that you stop living—and with the right retirement plan, it can be the beginning of the best years of your life.

Find yourself a financial advisor, one that specializes in the area of retirement income planning that you are comfortable with and sit down with them. Discuss the things you have learned about in these pages and start to optimize the money that you have—for the life that you want in retirement.

To your retirement!

- Diane Marra

References
Chapter 1

Retirement Quotes
http://www.brainyquote.com/quotes/keywords/retirement.html

Don't let Inflation Ruin Retirement
http://www.bambrose.com/blog/dont-let-inflation-ruin-retirement/

Rowland, Ron, *Four Risks That Could Ruin Your Retirement*
http://www.forbes.com/sites/investor/2010/04/26/four-risks-that-could-ruin-your-retirement/

Make Economic Security In Retirement A Personal Responsibility
http://www.publicagendaarchives.org/discussion-guides/make-economic-security-retirement-personal-responsibility

Era Of Personal Responsibility For Retirement Planning Brings Hope
http://ourvoice.thegazettecompany.com/2014/08/era-of-personal-responsibility-for-retirement-planning-brings-hope/

Brandon, Emily, *The Growing Challenge Of Funding Retirement*
http://money.usnews.com/money/retirement/articles/2012/02/01/the-growing-challenge-of-funding-retirement

Majority Of Workers Feel Responsible To Save For Their Retirement
http://www.limra.com/Posts/PR/News_Releases/Majority_of_Workers_Feel_Responsible_To_Save_For_Their_Retirement.aspx

Haskins, Ron, *The Sequence Of Personal Responsibility*
http://www.brookings.edu/research/articles/2009/07/09-responsibility-haskins

Brown, Jeffrey, *Reasons To Be Wary Of State-Run Retirement Plans*
http://www.forbes.com/sites/jeffreybrown/2014/02/10/state-run-retirement-plans/

The Retirement Shift: From Accumulation To Distribution
http://stancorpadvisers.com/the-retirement-shift-from-accumulation-to-distribution/

Krooks, Bernard, A, *The Five Phases Of Retirement Planning*
http://www.forbes.com/sites/bernardkrooks/2011/02/16/the-five-phases-of-retirement-planning/

Bastow, Mark, *Adjust To A Changing Retirement Landscape*
http://investorplace.com/2013/06/adjust-to-a-changing-retirement-landscape-tlt-tip/#.VDn4DfmSySo

Hedging 7 Big Retirement Risks
http://www.bankrate.com/finance/retirement/hedging-7-big-retirement-risks-1.aspx

Five Retirement Income Risks And How To Help Avoid Them
http://www.principal.com/planningcenter/retirementplanning/retirementincome/retirementnews/fiveretirementincomerisks.htm

Chapter 2

Retirement Quotes
http://www.brainyquote.com/quotes/keywords/retirement.html

Set Up A Retirement Income Plan
https://personal.vanguard.com/us/insights/retirement/living/retirement-income-withdrawal-strategy

Planning Retirement
http://www.ziegler.com/wealth-management/financial-planning/retirement-income-planning/

Brooks, Rodney, *Creating A Plan For The Right Retirement Income*
http://www.usatoday.com/story/money/columnist/brooks/2014/02/25/retirement-retire-pension-401k-financial-planner/5584791/

12 Key Questions Every Retiree Must Answer
http://artifexfinancial.com/12-key-questions-every-retiree-must-answer/

Powell, Robert, *12 Questions To Answer Before You Retire*
http://www.marketwatch.com/story/12-questions-to-answer-before-you-
retire-2013-02-28

Begany, Tim, *Top 10 Tips For A Financially Safe Retirement*
http://www.investopedia.com/articles/retirement/10/10-tips-for-safe-retirement.asp

Strategies For Building A Laddered Retirement Portfolio
https://www.biechele-royce.com/873819.pdf

The Best Passive Retirement Strategy In The World
http://seekingalpha.com/article/2287813-the-best-passive-retirement-strategy-in-the-
world

Strategic Asset Allocation
http://www.investopedia.com/terms/s/strategicassetallocation.asp

Van Bergen, Jason, *6 Asset Allocation Strategies That Work*
http://www.investopedia.com/articles/04/031704.asp

Mistakes To Avoid: Not Monitoring Your Financial Progress And Measuring Results
http://www.bbt.com/bbtdotcom/financial-education/savings/not-monitoring-
progress.page

Balancing Cash Flow And Retirement Goals
http://www.raymondjames.com/paramount/pdfs/balancing_cash_flows.pdf

Laddering, http://en.wikipedia.org/wiki/Laddering

Chapter 3

Famous Retirement Quotes
http://www.newretirement.com/Planning101/Thoughts_On_Retirement.aspx

Risk Tolerance
http://www.investopedia.com/terms/r/risktolerance.asp

Marquit, Miranda, *What's Your Risk Tolerance?*
http://money.usnews.com/money/blogs/the-smarter-mutual-fund-
investor/2013/04/02/whats-your-risk-tolerance

Smith, Ralph, *Calculating the 2015 Cost Of Living Adjustment (COLA)*
http://www.fedsmith.com/2014/06/18/calculating-the-2015-cost-of-living-adjustment-cola/

Hawkins, Ken, *Common Risks That Can Ruin Your Retirement*
http://www.investopedia.com/articles/retirement/08/post-retirement-risks-outlive-assets.asp

Kaplan, Eve, *Can You Afford Retirement?* http://www.forbes.com/sites/feeonlyplanner/2012/09/17/can-you-afford-retirement/

Calculating Your Retirement Income Needs
http://www.sunlife.ca/Canada/ataglance/Library/RRSP+-+Retirement+Savings/Retirement+income+needs?vgnLocale=en_CA

10 Steps To A Retirement Action Plan (Part 1)
http://www.kramerwealth.com/10-steps-to-a-retirement-action-plan-part-1/

Holsopple, Scott, *7 Steps To Reach Your Retirement Goals*
http://money.usnews.com/money/blogs/the-smarter-mutual-fund-investor/2012/01/24/7-steps-to-reach-your-retirement-goals

Sequencing Asset Liquidation – Which Retirement Assets Should You Use First?
http://www.myretirementpaycheck.org/savings-investments/sequencing-asset-liquidation.aspx

Reinhold, Eric, *Which Retirement Assets Should You Withdraw First?*
http://www.cbn.com/finance/which-retirement-assets-should-you-withdraw-first.aspx

Blankenshop, Jim, *Which Retirement Account Should You Tap First?*
http://www.forbes.com/sites/advisor/2011/05/03/which-account-should-you-tap-first/

Outcome Oriented Investing
https://www.russell.com/uk/files/russellinvestments_outcomeoriented-casestudysalesaid.pdf

Chapter 4

The Retirement Quotes Café
http://www.retirement-quotes.com/

Mayo, Andy, *Protecting Your Retirement Assets*
http://www.investopedia.com/articles/financial-theory/08/risk-ruin.asp

Prior, Anna, *Making Your Retirement Assets Last*
http://online.wsj.com/articles/SB10000872396390443991704577578860843781548

Asset Allocation
http://www.investopedia.com/terms/a/assetallocation.asp

Miller, Scott, G, *10 Most Common Asset Protection Planning Mistakes*
http://www.broadandcassel.com/pubdetails.aspx?ID=5980

Nawrocki, Nancy, C, *10 Asset Protection Planning Mistakes*
http://www.nawrockilaw.com/10-Asset-Protection-Planning-Mistakes-PDF.pdf

Cussen, Mark, P, *Top 7 Estate Planning Mistakes*
http://www.investopedia.com/articles/retirement/08/estate-planning-mistakes.asp

Asset Allocation Calculator
http://www.bankrate.com/calculators/retirement/asset-allocation.aspx

Mayo, Andy, *Protecting Your Retirement Assets*
http://www.investopedia.com/articles/financial-theory/08/risk-ruin.asp

Manage Retirement Assets
https://content.sharefc.com/sites/client/wells/wfs/category.vm?topic=6064

7 Ways To stretch Your Retirement Income
**http://www.bankrate.com/finance/financial-literacy/7-ways-to-stretch-your-
retirement-income-3.aspx**

Chapter 5

www.dmarra.incomeforlife.com

www.marrafinancialgroup.com

Chapter 6

Retirement Quotes
http://www.brainyquote.com/quotes/keywords/retirement.html

http://irs.gov

What Is A 401(k)?
http://guides.wsj.com/personal-finance/retirement/what-is-a-401k/

What Is A 401(k) Plan? A Quick Overview
http://www.401khelpcenter.com/401k_defined.html#.VK4eiCuUeSo

Stoffel, Brian, *The Average American Has This Much Saved In A 401(K) -- How Do You Compare?*
http://www.fool.com/investing/general/2015/01/05/the-average-american-has-this-much-saved-in-a-401k.aspx

Ciaran, John, *Can An Employee Roll Over A 401 (K) Into A Self-Directed IRA While Still Employed?*
http://finance.zacks.com/can-employee-roll-over-401k-selfdirected-ira-still-employed-7336.html

Self-Directed IRA
http://en.wikipedia.org/wiki/Self-directed_IRA

Stretch IRA
http://www.investopedia.com/terms/s/stretch-ira.asp

Jacobs, Deborah, L, *How To Stretch Out An IRA*
http://www.forbes.com/2010/05/04/stretch-ira-roth-estate-taxes-personal-finance-deborah-jacobs.html

Spiegelman, Rande, *Stretching Your IRA: Transferring Wealth To The Next Generation*
http://www.schwab.com/public/schwab/nn/articles/Stretching-Your-IRA-Transferring-Wealth-to-the-Next-Generation

What Is The Stretch IRA Strategy/ https://www.wealthmanagement.ml.com/Publish/Content/application/pdf/GWMOL/Stretch-IRA-Strategy_090712.pdf

Taulli, Tom, *How To Roll Over Your 401(k) To An IRA Without Stress*
http://investorplace.com/2012/05/how-to-roll-over-401k-ira-rollover/#.VK5LaSuUeSo

Pendykoski, Rick, *Implication Of Self-Directed Rollover – 401(K) To IRA & IRA To 401(K)*
http://seekingalpha.com/instablog/4604201-rickpendykoski/1042561-implications-of-self-directed-rollover-401-k-to-ira-and-ira-to-401-k

Self-Directed IRA A Good Bet?

http://www.bankrate.com/finance/retirement/self-directed-ira-a-good-bet-1.aspx

Chapter 7

Retire Quotes
http://www.brainyquote.com/quotes/keywords/retire.html

Developing A "Tax-Smart" Retirement Income Strategy
https://www.putnam.com/literature/pdf/II866.pdf

Tax Free Retirement Income Strategies
https://www.financialhealth.co/index.php/retire-smarter/tax-free-retirement-income-strategies

Smart IRA Withdrawal Strategies
https://www.fidelity.com/viewpoints/retirement/smart-ira-withdrawal-strategies

Cussen, Mark P, *How Can I Fund A Roth IRA If My Income Is Too High To Make Direct Contributions?*
http://www.investopedia.com/ask/answers/042214/how-can-i-fund-roth-ira-if-my-income-too-high-make-direct-contributions.asp

Garland, Susan, B, *Tap An IRA Early*
Delay Social Security
http://www.kiplinger.com/article/retirement/T051-C000-S004-tap-an-ira-early-delay-social-security.html

Keebler, Robert, E, *Using Roth IRA Distributions To Mitigate Income Taxes And Enhance Overall Wealth: Part 1,*
http://tax.cchgroup.com/images/FOT/JORP_03-10_Keebler.pdf

Johnson, Charlotte, *How To Calculate Provisional Income*
http://wiki.fool.com/How_to_Calculate_Provisional_Income

Provisional Income
http://www.investopedia.com/terms/p/provisional-income.asp

Understanding Fixed Index Annuities
https://www2.allianzlife.com/IIG/Content/Documents/Forms_And_Marketing_
Materials/SalesTools/M-5217.pdf

Traditional IRAs: Distributions
http://www.investopedia.com/university/retirementplans/ira/ira3.asp

Withdrawing From Your IRA.
https://www.fidelity.com/retirement-planning/learn-about-iras/ira-withdrawal

Chapter 8

Favorite Estate Planning Quotes
http://indianwellsestateplanningattorney.com/2013/02/25/favorite-estate-planning-
quotes-1/

The Learn Vest Staff, *Estate Planning Your Need-To-Know*
http://www.forbes.com/sites/learnvest/2013/05/24/estate-planning-your-need-to-
know/

A Beginners Guide To Estate Planning
http://www.ritchiecastellan.com.au/Sites/283/Images%20Files/Beginners%20
Guide%20to%20Estate%20Planning.pdf

10 Income And Estate Planning Strategies For 2015
https://www.putnam.com/literature/pdf/II922.pdf

Coombes, Andrea, *4 Estate-Plan Strategies For Boomers*
http://www.marketwatch.com/story/5-estate-plan-strategies-for-boomers-2013-11-29

Ten Benefits Of Estate Planning For You And Your Loved Ones
http://morristrust.com/2012/03/ten-benefits-of-estate-planning-for-you-and-your-
loved-ones/

10 Reasons To Create An Estate Plan Now
http://www.elderlawanswers.com/10-reasons-to-create-an-estate-plan-now-1076

Chapter 9

Marotta, David John, *The False Promises Of Annuities And Annuity Calculators*
http://www.forbes.com/sites/davidmarotta/2012/08/27/the-false-promises-of-annuities-and-annuity-calculators/

Are Variable Annuities A Good Investment?
http://www.wsj.com/articles/SB10001424052702303916904577376193314287640

Variable Annuities: Beyond The Hard Sell
http://www.finra.org/Investors/ProtectYourself/InvestorAlerts/AnnuitiesAndInsurance/
P005976

Variable Annuities
http://www.sec.gov/investor/pubs/sec-guide-to-variable-annuities.pdf

The Risk Of Variable Annuities
http://www.rothira.com/blog/the-risk-of-variable-annuities

Ultimate Guide To Retirement – What Is A Fixed Annuity?
http://money.cnn.com/retirement/*guide*/annuities_fixed.moneymag/

Explaining Types Of Fixed Annuities
http://www.investopedia.com/articles/retirement/05/071205.asp

Fixed Annuity
http://www.investopedia.com/terms/f/fixedannuity.asp

3 Risk Of Purchasing A Fixed Annuity
http://www.moneycrashers.com/what-is-fixed-income-annuity-definition-pros-cons/

3 Risks Of Purchasing A Fixed Annuity
http://money.usnews.com/money/blogs/on-retirement/2010/12/16/3-risks-of-purchasing-a-fixed-annuity

6 Questions Before Buying A Fixed Indexed Annuity
http://www.cbsnews.com/news/six-questions-to-ask-before-buying-a-fixed-indexed-annuity/

Haithcock, Stan, *Behind The Indexed Annuity Curtain*
http://www.marketwatch.com/story/behind-the-indexed-annuity-curtain-2013-01-14

Fixed Indexed Annuities – Growth Potential Based On A Market Index, http://www.
nationwide.com/fixed-indexed-annuities.jsp

What Are The Differences Between Fixed And Variable Annuities? http://www.irionline.
org/consumer-articles/what-are-the-differences-between-fixed-and-variable-annuities-

Chapter 10

Social Security Quotes
http://www.brainyquote.com/quotes/keywords/social_security.html

Garland, Susan, B, *Strategies To Boost Your Social Security*
http://www.kiplinger.com/article/retirement/T051-C000-S004-strategies-to-boost-
your-social-security.html

Mahaney, James, *Innovative Strategies To Help Maximize Social Security Benefits*
http://research.prudential.com/documents/rp/InnovativeSocialSecurityNov2012.pdf

Social Security Benefits
http://www.ssa.gov/oact/cola/Benefits.html

Primary Insurance Amount
http://www.ssa.gov/oact/cola/piaformula.html

Dowd, Casey, *You Could Live To 100: How To Plan For A Long Retirement*
http://www.foxbusiness.com/personal-finance/2014/06/26/could-live-to-100-how-to-
plan-for-long-retirement/

Hopkins, Jamie, *Planning For An Uncertain Life Expectancy In Retirement*
http://www.forbes.com/sites/jamiehopkins/2014/02/03/planning-for-an-uncertain-
life-expectancy-in-retirement/

Plan For A Long Retirement
https://personal.vanguard.com/us/insights/retirement/plan-for-a-long-retirement-tool

Block, Sandra, *Best Social Security Strategies For Married Couples*
http://www.kiplinger.com/article/retirement/T051-C000-S002-social-security-
strategies-for-married-couples.html

Social Security For Married Couples, http://www.aarp.org/content/dam/aarp/money/
investing/2014-04/social-security-for-married-couples-aarp.pdf

Retirement Planner: Benefits For Your Divorced Spouse
http://www.ssa.gov/retire2/yourdivspouse.htm

Social Security Tips For Singles
https://www.fidelity.com/viewpoints/retirement/social-security-tips-for-singles

Hinden, Stan, *Social Security Survivor Benefits*
http://www.aarp.org/work/social-security/info-02-2011/social_security_mailbox_survivor_benefits.html

Chapter 11

Social Security Quotes
http://www.brainyquote.com/quotes/keywords/social_security.html

http://www.dmarra.sswise.com

Saletta, Chuck, *3 Reasons To Delay Your Social Security*
http://www.fool.com/retirement/general/2014/08/08/3-reasons-to-delay-your-social-security.aspx

Should You Delay Taking Social Security Until You're 70?
http://www.wsj.com/articles/SB10001424052702304275304579392832120521694

Cussen, Mark, P, *Avoid the Social Security Tax Trap*
http://www.investopedia.com/articles/pf/08/social-security-tax.asp

Are Social Security Benefits Taxable Income? http://www.efile.com/social-security-taxable-income-tax-benefits/

Social Security Understanding The Benefits
http://ssa.gov/pubs/EN-05-10024.pdf

Hinden, Stan, *Are My Social Security Benefits Taxable?*
http://www.aarp.org/work/social-security/info-2014/social-security-benefit-taxes.html'

Survivor's Planner: How Much Would Your Benefit Be?
http://www.ssa.gov/survivorplan/ifyou5.htm

Martin, Ray, *Understanding Social Security Survivor Benefits*
http://www.cbsnews.com/news/understanding-social-security-survivor-benefits/

Siedle, Edward, *The Greatest Retirement Crisis In American History*
http://www.forbes.com/sites/edwardsiedle/2013/03/20/the-greatest-retirement-crisis-in-american-history/

Chapter 12

Care Quotes, **http://www.brainyquote.com/quotes/keywords/care_2.html**

www.morningstar.com

IMPORTANT NOTE

Website's addresses can change and websites or page sometimes are deleted or moved. All of these links were active at the time of publication.

Index

About the Author

Diane Marra is an Independent Registered Financial Consultant and Investment Advisor Representative for a Registered Investment Advisory firm. She began her career in 1982. She is committed to empowering retirees, as well as people nearing retirement, with the knowledge necessary to make more informed decisions about their financial well-being and successful retirement. Diane offers her clients vast experience with and knowledge of retirement issues, which she gained over 31 years in the financial services industry.

Diane specializes in providing planning and guidance for those who seek to maintain or create a better lifestyle in retirement, while emphasizing an investment management system designed to create low-risk, low-volatility portfolios. She has helped many individuals and couples at all economic levels enjoy a worry-free retirement, knowing that their money is safe and ready for them when needed.

Over the years, Diane has been a member of various financial organizations, including the International Association of Registered Financial Consultants, the Society of Certified Senior Advisors, the National Association of Insurance and Financial Advisors, the National Association of Life Underwriters. and a student of the life Underwriter Training Council. She is also an approved member in good standing with the National Ethics Association.

Diane has lectured in the Tri-State area on financial topics important to individuals, groups and organizations, both pre-and post-retirement. She has also been registered as an instructor for the Richness of Life Institute, which teaches financial education courses.

Diane was born and raised on Long Island in New York, where she still lives with her husband Paul and their three children. They enjoy time outdoors and spend much of their free time together in upstate New York. She has spent 13 years as a volunteer paramedic for the Suffolk County Emergency Medical Service, donating much of her time to those in need of immediate medical attention.

www.ingramcontent.com/pod-product-compliance
Lightning Source LLC
Chambersburg PA
CBHW042311210326
41598CB00041B/7349